Marketing Strategies for Growth in Uncertain Times

Allan J. Magrath

Marketing Strategies for Growth in Uncertain Times

Foreword by Anthony Rutigliano
Editor/Publisher, *Sales and Marketing Management* magazine

Printed on recyclable paper

AMERICAN MARKETING ASSOCIATION
American Marketing Association
Chicago, Illinois

NTC Business Books
a division of *NTC Publishing Group* • Lincolnwood, Illinois USA

Library of Congress Cataloging-in-Publication Data

Magrath, Allan J.
Marketing strategies for growth in uncertain times / Allan J. Magrath.
p. cm.
ISBN 0-0442-3323-4
1. Marketing. I. Title.
HF5415.M2679 1995
658.8—dc20 94-20721
CIP

Published in conjunction with the American Marketing Association, 250 South Wacker Drive, Chicago, Illinois, 60606.

Published by NTC Business Books, a division of NTC Publishing Group
4255 West Touhy Avenue
Lincolnwood (Chicago), Illinois 60606-1975, U.S.A.

Manufactured in the United States of America.

Contents

Chapter 3

Growing in Mature Markets

Chapter 4

Growth Through Brand Extension

Chapter 5

Growing Through Services

Chapter 6

Growing Through Collaboration

Epilogue

The Growth Masters

Dedication

For Dr. William E. Coyne, a great leader and a great person—
in other words, a helluva combination

Foreword

Anthony J. Rutigliano
Publisher, *Sales & Marketing Management*

At a recent meeting of marketing professionals, a speaker asked how many of the more than one hundred executives gathered were accountable to their bosses for generating sales leads. It was rather astonishing, even to members of the audience, that only three of the marketing executives raised their hands. Further questioning revealed that the gap between marketing and sales was even wider when it came to such matters as setting goals and communicating strategies.

What's going on here?

In these difficult days of intense competition and ever-shorter product lives, the need for marketing to be a strategic partner of sales and many other departments is greater than ever. Yet, at many companies, marketing remains the most ivory-towered department, secure in its lack of accountability, but perhaps less effective because of it.

We've all heard corporate and advertising agency executives apply the term *good marketing* to campaigns and strategies that failed to move product out of the warehouse. Similarly, many of us have heard these same executives knock the opinions of sales and service personnel whose job it is to know what the customer wants.

Sometimes it's easy to imagine how so many companies have devolved to this way of doing things. Corporate executives have allowed marketing to dance to a different beat because they don't understand it. And how could they when so many marketing successes seem to fly in the face of common sense?

For instance, line extensions seem to make perfectly good sense, giving companies the opportunity to play off the success of a product, its reputation, and an established and happy distribution channel. However, the failures that have resulted from attempts to simply repeat success are innumerable and often embarrassing. Xerox twice tried to reproduce its success in copiers to become an office systems company and failed miserably and expensively both times. For years, Volkswagen has attempted to capitalize on its earlier success in the inexpensive auto market by producing a wider line of higher priced cars and as a result has been all but driven out of the U.S. And Federal Express brazenly thought it could capitalize on its success in the States to become a worldwide carrier, but the payoff from this costly adventure is still in the mail.

At the same time, Marriott Hotels has successfully launched new brands of transient and long-term-stay properties with eventual success. Baxter Travenol has become all things to almost all hospitals to grow into one of the leaders in the burgeoning health care market. And 3M hardly becomes unglued when it extends its lines in everything from office products to surgical supplies. Is it any wonder that marketing executives talk to themselves?

Helping *Sales and Marketing Management* keep such developments in perspective has been Allan J. Magrath, a columnist for us on the subject of marketing for many years. And in this book, Allan distills many of the great success stories of these uncertain times to convey valuable lessons in marketing and corporate strategy.

What characterizes this business age more than any other is the need for rapid development of products and services and almost immediate market penetration. To achieve these ends, companies must have greater precision in the development of their marketing plans, the management of their sales territories, the control of their budgets, and the calculation of their inventory levels. They must maintain a focus on their core business, looking for ways to capitalize on it, while being mindful that to confuse customers about what they are is to lose them.

Businesses must stay close to their customers, soliciting their help in the design of new products and services. They must look for ways to embed their technologies and systems at client firms so that life without them becomes unimaginable for the customer. In this comprehensive book, Allan gives us winning examples of these and other strategies.

In these pages you will read about companies that have successfully introduced new products and created entire new categories and niches, how companies have used design to win new markets in both products and services and how market research and even customer complaints been used effectively to shape those new offerings. While new products are certainly the most exciting marketing events, Magrath tells us how fortunes have been made through customization of everything from connectors to golf clubs.

Magrath informs us that all companies must constantly respond to their customers, those customers's needs and their locations. Tracking those three market basics accurately will help marketers find new users, develop complementary products, find new bases on which to compete, develop new uses for tried and true products. Having an ear to the ground also will help companies find the right way to position leading-edge products, integrate new markets, and find fertile soil for continued expansion.

Is yours a mature market? This book will tell you how to stage an all-out assault for market-share growth, how to stay on top of your competitors, and how to redefine your market to find competitive openings, whether these be share of mind, share of shelf, share of technology, or share of selling effort. As a marketing general at your company it's up to you to pick the fight that you can win and develop a strategy for success. In addition, Magrath examines other effective growth strategies such as partnering, licensing and, yes, even line extensions.

This book is full of anecdotes and case studies in marketing success, the stuff that made Magrath's column for our magazine popular for so long. One of my favorites involves the much-derided U.S. auto industry, which is now on the comeback trail after giving up so much of its market to foreign competitors. Magrath tells us that when conducting research on new products, the Japanese often deemphasize formal data collection in favor of personal observation of actual and potential customers. For instance, Japanese auto makers regularly send their designers to watch women getting in and out of cars and to watch them drive so they can assess the female-friendliness of their designs. In contrast, during the 1970s and 1980s, when the Japanese were preying upon their market, Big Three executives failed to notice because everyone they knew drove Lincolns, Cadillacs and Fifth Avenues.

Who are your customers? What other needs of theirs can your company satisfy? How can you make it difficult or more undesirable for your customers to do business with anyone else? How can you make it easier for them to do business with you? How can you best meet the challenges of your competitors? In what other ways can your existing products be used? These are just some of the questions that this book should prompt you to ask yourself and those you work with at the company. The answers will provide a solid marketing strategy for these turbulent times.

Preface

Control is easy. Organizing marketing for growth is hard.

Barrie Berg
Principal
Booz-Allen, Hamilton, Inc.
London, U.K.

Growth—both how to get it and how to keep it going with astute strategic choices and nimble execution—is *the* business issue of the 1990s. The unique challenge of the present is achieving Sustainable Quality Growth without the benefit of price increases amidst enormously tough market conditions where customers are increasingly demanding, markets are maturing, and competitors are unrelenting. This book is about ways to achieve that Sustainable Quality Growth—increases in both top-line sales and bottom-line profits, and it is about companies that have produced that remarkable achievement over considerable periods of time, that have achieved double-digit sales growth for five or more years and solid profits to go with those sales increases.

A "remarkable achievement"? Yes, because as Barrie Berg points out, unlocking fresh growth opportunities has been extraordinarily difficult in recent years, and it's unlikely to get any easier in the future. The evidence for this statement is everywhere. Just when you think you've found the "magic formula" for achieving growth, the wheels can fall off. Japanese car makers' sales and profits are off as Detroit's Big Three fight back, Japan's home market softens, and the yen's value explodes.

And this is not an aberration occurring in a mature industry. Microsoft and all the other software makers, from Lotus to Borland, WordPerfect, and Software Publishing Corp., have been stopped short in their growth tracks by price wars. Unit volume is up, but margins and revenue growth are way off. Even a firm that dominates in industry share can find its efforts for sustainable quality growth thwarted. Boeing dominates large aircraft sales, but with its customers losing money and cutbacks in defense spending, its order books are suffering as it scrambles to cut its costs and plane prices. Merck, the world's leading drug maker, has had to adjust to pressures on its revenues from health care cost containment and buy Medco—a mail order drug distribution firm. Even Disney, which for many years has had the Midas touch, is in deep trouble with major losses at EuroDisney, where customer attendance is below break-even operating costs.

Business Response

Firms have responded to discontinuous market, consumer, and industry change by transforming themselves, attempting to sustain the quality growth that in more stable growing times came more easily. As marketing advantages have become tougher to come by, companies have addressed the problem of growth in sales and earnings by reconfiguring their total business systems. Every potential differentiating advantage is being re-examined from innovation, to cost, distribution channels, speed of response, customer service, product quality, branding, overseas sales—you name it. For instance, McDonald's has altered its menu (breakfast, pizza), its meal systems (more drive-thrus, home delivery), its locations (many nontraditional sites in airports, baseball stadiums, inside retail store chains, in hospitals, theme parks, at army bases and inside universities), its market reach (in China, Russia, Poland, and other emerging markets), its franchisee relations (regional councils), and its pricing (value-meals now dominate transactions). Yet the company will still be hard-pressed to hit the double-digit sales growth it attained in the 1980s.

Bottom-line growth is just as elusive as top-line sales increases. Compaq redesigned most of its product line and reengineered its costs much lower, yet its margins earned on 1992 sales of $4 billion were only half of what they were in 1990 on sales of $3.5 billion.

Put simply, traditional formulas aren't working the way they did in the past. History may show that the 1990s challenged firms to alter growth formulas in ways never envisioned. And the winning companies that are around in the next century may resemble themselves in name only, relative to what they were in the 1980s. Certainly, General Motors and IBM already would attest to this, as will Bell Atlantic, Chrysler, AT&T, Merck, and Royal Dutch Shell. As Sir Peter Holmes has stated (in *Fortune*):

> In good weather, even the less fit climb well—but when rain turns to snow, good climbers keep going and the mediocre turn back.

Climbing ahead—growing—in the 1990s has been and will continue to be more treacherous but just as vital as ever, since using price increases as a way to grow companies has been all but eliminated in most markets. Inflation has turned to deflation with wholesale producer prices less than 1 percent in 1993 and below 2 percent since 1990.

Why Sustainable Quality Growth Is So Important

Sustainable Quality Growth is the elixir of business health—and of societal health in general. A string of positive results occur when firms grow in sustained, profitable ways:

1. *Financially,* as earnings and sales increase, companies can self-finance their operations and avoid crippling debt. Shareholder value is a function of the cash dividend paid on a share plus the common stock's price appreciation. For the majority of stocks in North America only 25 percent of total shareholder value comes from cash dividends. The other 75 percent flows from price appreciation, which is the *market's capitalization estimate*

of how the firm will grow in the future. Without future growth, a firm's stock does not appreciate. In fact, the only way firms not growing can keep stock prices up is by boosting their cash dividend payouts. Unfortunately, the higher the dividend paid, the less cash from operations is left for financing future growth opportunities. So growth is critical to both paying cash dividends and financing the firm's future expansion, which drives its shareholder value.

2. *Employees* of growing, profitable firms eschew pride, providing positive word of mouth advertising for the firm, which help the company attract the best new employees from various talent pools. Employees in such firms are usually better challenged with interesting work and above-average pay as the company forges ahead, expanding its horizons and the problems and opportunities it tackles.
3. *End-User Customers* of companies with stellar reputations for growth and innovative opportunity exploitation boost their customer retention, since these customers are attracted to the firm's vitality and stature. Customers want to partner with high-vitality, growing profitable corporations to gain the benefits from the company's new products and innovative services.
4. *Communities* in which growing profitable firms exist benefit from better tax revenues and construction activity flowing to local contractors.
5. *Distributors, Dealers, or Retailers* who provide access to end-user customers for a growing company often provide the supplier with preferential sales support since they are making healthy profits from the company's offerings. And these trade channels will usually be quick to list the firms' new offerings, on the assumption that they too will sell well.

6. *Vendors* who supply the growing, profitable company benefit from growth in demand for their parts, components, raw materials, or packaging supplies while knowing the firm's healthy profits mean that they will get paid on time, something near and dear to their company treasurers.
7. *Governments* often listen most closely to successful growing enterprises, looking to them to assist in developing market opportunities, both foreign and domestic.
8. *Managements* of growing profitable companies have less turmoil in the ranks, which so often finds its genesis in poor operating results, shareholder unhappiness, and employee unrest. Indeed, from a strategic point of view, managers of successful enterprises tend to have strategic choices often not available to weakly financed companies, whose cash flow situations restrict their capital investment spending, marketing, and manufacturing options.

Marketing Strategies for Growth

In this book I identify 18 different ways to grow and demonstrate how high-performance firms employ these different strategies. These 18 different growth vectors flow from 6 basic strategy platforms:

1. New Products
2. New Markets
3. Share Taking
4. Merchandising, Licensing and Flanker Brands
5. Added Services
6. Acquisitions/Joint Venture/Alliances

Each of the six chapters of the book elaborate on the variants of these six strategic platforms. For instance, new products are dissected into new "category creating" products, customized new products, and new product portfolio-broadening. Similarly, new markets break out into new users, new usages, and new locales (going international or into neglected parts of the market). Added services involve "systems selling," turn-key services, and other value-added service positioning.

At a time when companies cannot increase their prices, it is vital for them to understand these strategies. Those companies discussed in this book have no connecting thread as to their line of business, size, complexity or location. Some, such as Disney Co., are well known while others, such as Crompton and Knowles (one of the world leaders in specialty chemicals such as apparel dyes), are not. Some, such as Molex, are high tech, while others are distinctly low tech, such as Fruit-of-the-Loom. Some are mass marketers such as Swatch while others, like Karsten Manufacturing (makers of Ping Golf Clubs), work away in niches. Almost all have mastered the art of growing for sustained periods while maintaining their corporate profitability.

In total I've dissected 175 companies in 35 different industries, from firms making miniature ball bearings (Minebea) to those manufacturing drapery hardware (Newell Co.) or hospital supplies (Baxter). Included are in-depth looks at great growth mastering companies using each of the different platforms to achieve their ends. These include Ford Mazda in automobiles, Key Corp in banking, Toys R Us in retailing, Baxter is health care, Betz Labs in chemicals, Elan PLC in drug delivery systems, Starter Corp in sports apparel licensing and Thorn EMI in the music recording and publishing business.

Not all the examples used are large companies, as I've included a look at Leegin Leather, a belt manufacturer; Wabash National, a truck trailer supplier; Pick-Point Sports, a golf ball maker; and Renishaw PLC, a precision instrument firm.

The Formula for the Future

The past 15 years have witnessed major dislocations and changes in the ways organizations conduct their businesses and earn a profit, as companies have struggled to adapt to the sea-changes in economic and market conditions. They have come under various names—reengineering, downsizing, and so forth—but they have had one thing in common: scaling back in the face of uncertainty. And while much of the suffering and turmoil has been necessary to correct the excesses of the past and to adjust to very different circumstances of the present, by themselves they are limited. The path to future prosperity of society in general and business in particular requires growth.

Bob Nourse, CEO of the Bombay Company, knows the perils and potential of growing in the face of uncertainty. This North American retailer began his company in 1980 with a single store, but by 1994 it had grown to 445 stores doing $320 million in sales and producing annual double-digit earnings per share *increases.* As he said in the *Business Quarterly:*

> Risk is where opportunities to earn money are. The job in growing a company is to manage risk.

Navigating risks to find daylight in markets is what this book is about.

Chapter 1

Growing with New Products

Creating New Categories, Customized Products, and Expanded Portfolios

When it comes to new products, the large won't eat the small. The swift will eat the slow.

Robert Lutz
President, Chrysler
Forbes, Jan. 31, 1994, p. 126

Creating new products is one of the most exciting and potentially productive strategies for achieving profitable growth. History is filled with the stories of individuals of great imagination who conceived of breakthrough ideas to solve problems that, in some cases, the rest of the population only vaguely comprehended. Their innovation gave us electric light, the telephone, airplanes, refrigeration, personal computers, integrated circuits, photocopiers, television, and all manner of products around which entire industries have been built. That same spirit of innovation is evident in the leading companies of our time, and this chapter explores three key vectors of successful new product growth strategies.

The first strategy involves the creation of entirely new categories of products not seen before. Chrysler did this when it launched the minivan, an automobile with the utility of a truck and the comfort of a car. The second new product strategy is product customization—in effect, growing new products one customer or market segment at a time. This is the way many newspapers are published today—by customizing different editions with local news while retaining the core sections for their total readership. The third growth variant is creating portfolios of products that span the entire price/value spectrum. Pella Windows used to produce only expensive windows but expanded its portfolio with the PRO line of lower-cost windows for less-affluent customers who still wanted Pella's reliability.

What New Products Can Do

New products lift the morale of the sales force, preempt premium shelf space in distribution channels, excite customers, and often steal the advertising spotlight from older products. New products tend to take center stage in advertising because, being first to market, they avoid competitive comparisons and are less likely to get lost amid the general noise and promotional clutter of the marketplace. (For instance, the average television viewer sees 24 commercials per hour.) All of these tactical advantages can contribute to superior growth in revenue and outstanding profits.

Consider Kellogg's in the cereal business. Three of its key strategies as a firm are tied to new products. First, the company intends to grow its ready-to-eat cereal share in the U.S.; second, it wants to grow its global share of the cereal market; third, it wants to diversify beyond cereals into other food markets.

Kellogg's is utilizing new products to help it do all three. It is building U.S. share with Crispix, Nutri-Grain, and Marshmallow Krispies, products introduced in the late 1980s. It is increasing global share with Toasted Mini Wheats in Japan and Sustain, a new health-oriented cereal, in Australia. And in noncereal food markets, it has introduced Rice Krispies Snack Bars and Whitney's Yogurt.

Such strategies aren't limited to the retail food business. Gillette's Sensor razor and blades, launched in January 1990, accounted for $200 million in sales by year-end at an operating profit margin in excess of 33 percent. By 1991 it had captured 15 percent of both the American and European markets, reversing the company's stagnation and weak stock price. Prior to this new product Gillette's once-valuable brand name was being tarnished because its disposable razor systems were indistinguishable from competitors BIC and Schick. Gillette had become vulnerable to takeover and had fought off four separate takeover bids between 1986 and 1988. So, to a large extent its new product offering of Sensor may have saved the firm, allowing it to replenish its cash flow and go on to fund new strategic initiatives such as the purchase of Parker Pen to combine with its Paper Mate and Waterman brands.

Category Creation: Reshaping an Industry with New Products

If radical enough, a new product can reshape an entire industry. Howard Head (Prince Manufacturing) changed the tennis racket market forever in 1976, when he launched The Prince Classic, which had a head of 110 square inches versus the traditional 70 inches. This oversized head made it far easier for novices to learn tennis, while providing advanced players with more hitting power and fewer miscues. The traditional racket's share went from 100 percent in 1975 to 92 percent in 1978, then to less than 25 percent in 1984. By 1988, it was a mere 1 percent. So, in only ten years a single new product had completely revolutionized the business.

It is interesting to note that Wilson came along in 1988 and used a new product to change the tennis game once again. Its Profile "wide body" tennis racket had a 1½-inch-thick frame, twice the thickness of rackets such as the Prince Classic (hence its name). This new wide-body racket from Wilson captured $25 million in first-year revenues and established a new market for new wide-body racket styles. The Profile's hollow frame, made of lightweight materials, gave more power to the player, while absorbing greater shocks and lessening the chances of "tennis elbow" injuries.

In 1988, Japanese film manufacturer Fuji revolutionized the camera market by introducing the disposable camera, which attaches the lens to the film carrier rather than housing it and the film separately. Kodak quickly followed with its own disposable, the Fling 35, as the whole market shifted, with more than 21 million disposable cameras sold globally by 1988. Since that time, disposables have been improved with underwater capabilities and built-in telephoto lenses. This new product—the disposable camera—has created and defined a new market niche. It provides users greater ease of operation, lower cost, and greater convenience.

Niche Dominance by Design

New product design often has little or nothing to do with flashy packaging or high-style presentation. New design, as a means of winning new markets, can mean better performance. The Prince Classic, mentioned previously, is one example. The Ping golf club is another.

Karsten Manufacturing Corporation, of Phoenix, Arizona, has used new product design to create its distinctive Ping line of putters and golf clubs (irons). Karsten Solheim, the founder of Ping's line of clubs, conceived of the idea of a putter designed with more weight added to the heel and toe of the putter so that it would be easier to help keep the putter straight while stroking the ball (versus twisting in the golfer's hands and sending the ball off-course). So popular was this design innovation that the majority of golf pros switched to Ping putters in the sixties and seventies. As a result of this enormous popularity, Solheim applied new design ideas to irons as well, and since 1982 the company has sold more than one million sets of premium priced (30% over competitors) "Ping Eye 2" irons. All of this design emphasis has grown Karsten from next to nothing in 1960 to over $200 million in sales in 1992 and $80 million in pre-tax earnings.

Breakthroughs in Service Design

Design innovation as the foundation for new product entries is well established, but what is less well known is how dramatically this kind of innovation can propel a services-oriented company ahead of its competitors as well. In 1986 Citicorp reinvented the way many Americans select a mortgage. A new service, named Mortgage Power, united 3,000 real estate brokers, lawyers, and insurance agents into a 37-state referral network. The homebuyer who goes through an agent in the network can get a mortgage at a rate 1½ percent lower than that available from Citicorp directly. The agents in turn receive a broker's fee of one half of 1 percent from the homebuyer. So the agents win, as does the home buyer, and Citicorp gets the mortgage business. Citicorp markets Mortgage Power's convenience—hassle-free, minimum paperwork, guaranteed 15-day response where everybody wins—not its cost. Mortgage Power transformed Citicorp from a mortgage lender *not even among America's top 100* in 1981 to the nation's largest by 1990.

So a company redesigning a service—something as basic as obtaining a home mortgage—can achieve a competitive advantage and growth.

Case 1

Swatch: A Template for Creating and Dominating Niches

New products such as disposable cameras create new category niches. But, of course, to sustain growth a company must keep mining the niche, expanding it and dominating it. Otherwise the new product pioneer finds itself losing out to competitors, as did Sony, which pioneered the VCR niche with the Beta format but lost its leadership position to Matsushita's VHS format.

Swatch, a division of SMH Corp., of Biel, Switzerland, is a fine example of a firm whose new product created a niche that it subsequently has expanded and dominated. Swatch made low-cost quartz movement watches into fashion statements for the young. It was the first to target the youth market with colorful, emotionally charged, distinctively designed watches. In labs that turn out 140 new designs each year, Swatch has built a huge global niche for $40 watches with distinctive imagery, color combinations, and artwork created by world-class designers, painters, photographers, fashion experts, and artists. More than 27 million Swatches were sold in 1992, and in the fall of that year the firm celebrated the production of its 100 millionth watch since its founding.

The Swatch phenomenon represents a series of specific strategic steps. First, there was the creation of a radically different styled watch and watch band. Creation was followed by clever targeting to the twenty-something generation. Next, a selective distribution channel was set up, and then the niche was deepened by including many new models and a collector's series of limited-edition Swatches. With the addition of pricier watches (automatic and chronographic models), Swatch has further expanded distribution into fine jewelry stores in addition to its department store channels. More recently, the company has reinforced its powerful brand dominance and expanded its presence by adding other items to its mix of Swatch-branded products, including sunglasses and a watch-pager, called "Swatch-Piepser" (German for beeper), developed in conjunction with Mobil Comm. Exhibit 1–1 illustrates the Swatch niche dominance strategy.[1]

Swatch's success led to the turnaround of its parent, SMH, the Swiss Corporation for microelectronics and watch making, from a loss of $134 million in 1983 on sales of $1.1 billion to a profit of $286 million on sales of $2.1 billion in 1992. Swatch's success has increased the value of SMH's stock from 100 Swiss Francs in 1983 to 1,500 Swiss Francs in 1993.

The Swatch story illustrates three principles about growing with new products. First, such growth often starts with a clearly different and distinctly radical product concept (in this case, low-cost, high-style watches). Second, the

(Continued on next page)

idea needs constant freshening, as Swatch did by adding two new designer series of 70 models per series each year. Third, the product's distribution and advertising need to be well planned. Swatch created some channel exclusivity (despite the mass market appeal), and Swatch advertising has often been quite unusual, as evidenced by provocative marketing communications messages and images, such as its creation of a 500-foot-high, 13-ton, working Swatch model, positioned outside Frankfurt's tallest skyscraper, the headquarters of Commerzbank.

Exhibit 1–1
The Swatch Phenomenon

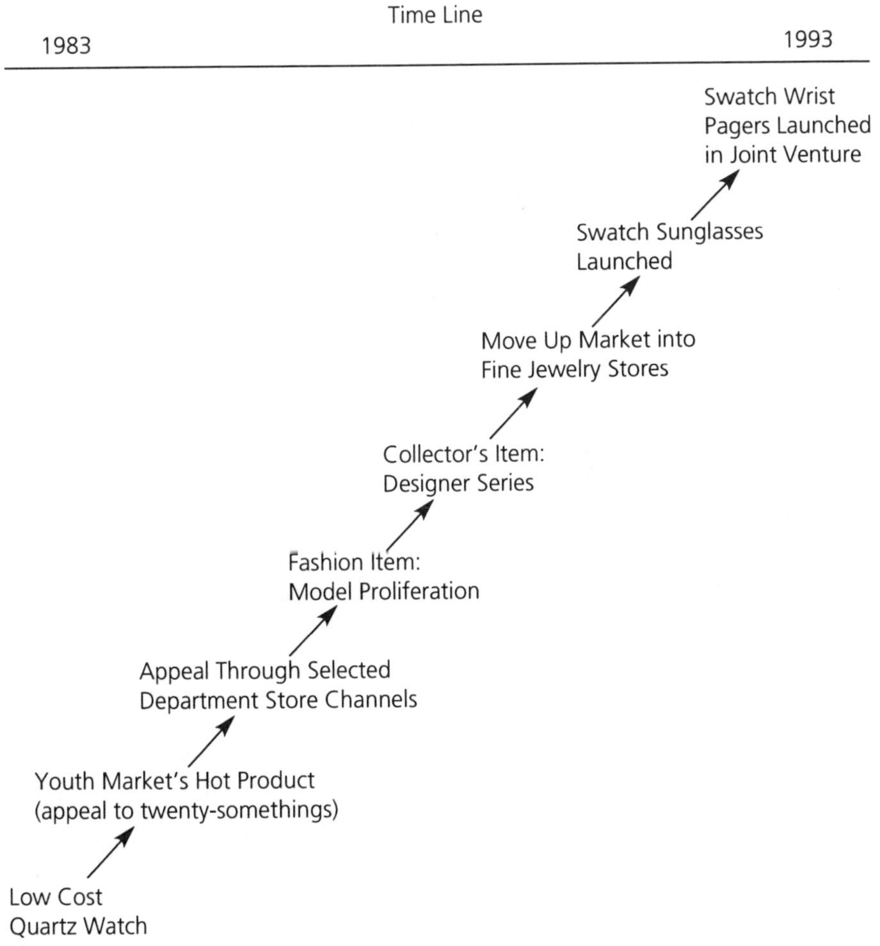

Listening to Customers: The Key to Success

The most fundamental and most overlooked ingredient for success in new product generation is immersion in one's market and in users'/customers' problems or concerns. Harley-Davidson executives routinely join motorcycle clubs to ride their products, hear complaints and concerns, and share insights about their motorcycles with other riders. In a very different product arena, Pratt and Whitney does the same thing. It sends design engineers to customer factories to see how its engines are fitted and how they perform once they have been assembled and put to work in their customers' products. And similar examples from all sorts of industries abound. For example, Karsten Solheim, the developer of the Ping putter, was himself a frustrated golfer, seeking an edge to improve his putting. And William Lear, the founder of Lear Jet, was an avid pilot long before he started and grew his own company. (Lear Jet is now owned by Bombardier.)

The approach to research used by many Japanese companies illustrates this point well. When conducting marketing research on new products, many Japanese companies deemphasize formal large-scale, data collection surveys in favor of personal observation of customers, both actual and potential. Japanese auto manufacturers regularly send their designers to watch women getting in and out of cars and to watch them driving in order to get to see whether their car designs are "woman-friendly." They feel that quantitative market surveys alone won't tell them whether to reposition a gear shift by two inches or change the shape of a window design for shorter people.[2] By way of contrast, during the 1970s and 1980s, when the Japanese were making serious inroads into the U.S. auto market, Big Three auto executives failed to notice the increasing prominence of Japanese autos. After all, everyone they knew drove American-made cars.

3M has a long track record of staying close to its users/customers when designing new products. Its new health care products for surgeons, dentists, operating room nurses, casting technicians, emergency room nurses, and other health care professionals are examples. 3M's Micropore brand tapes, Tegaderm brand dressings, Scotchcast casting material, Incise Surgical Drapes, and white fillings for teeth (P-50) owe their creation to such customer contacts.

New Problems in High Tech

In high-tech markets, growth from new products is more problematic than in markets where technology "churn" is lower. New high-tech products may have a very short life before displacement by the next generation's entry. Witness the computer industry, where minicomputers are giving way to personal computer networks, and personal computers to laptops and palm top units, all in the span of a few short years.

Timing the market invariably is the life-or-death marketing test for high-tech new products. For instance, in 1989, Canon launched the "Navigator," a combination PC, fax, phone, and printer and withdrew the product after several years of poor sales. In late 1994, Hewlett-Packard introduced a similar product. Although specific sales results were not available, initial prospects for success were positive. While market observers eventually may cite many factors contributing to the relative success and failure of these products, timing was undoubtedly the key differentiator.

High-tech new products also are higher risk in the sense that they are targeted to meet needs the customer may never have considered possible before, and which the customer *may* or *may not* view as important needs to fulfill. Kodak's disc camera miserably failed the all-important "needs test" on two scales: demand (at the time a strong market need was never established) and quality (it produced fuzzier pictures than customers would tolerate). Kodak is now betting a great deal on the success of its Photo CD system, which lets camera owners transfer snapshots to a digital disc for $20 per role and then, using a $400 player, display them on a television screen. But what if camera owners don't have a strong need for this, or don't own a television with sufficiently high resolution, or are willing to pay only $100 instead of the $400 it will cost to enjoy the product benefit? Will this type of high-tech product be a breakthrough, like Sony's Walkman or the video cassette recorder (VCR), or will it be a flop like the Disc camera?

In high-tech fields, multiple technologies often represent several ways of fulfilling the same need; and betting on which one will win out is a tough call. Wang bet that personal computers would not displace its word processors in office markets—and wound up in Chapter 11 bankruptcy proceedings because it guessed incorrectly. Xerox, on the other hand, bet that its high-speed Marathon copiers could replace some printing presses used in company in-plant print shops, and it won big in this market.

So, the gambles in high-tech new products are often major, and more unpredictable than in low-tech markets. A study by the Marketing Science Institute[3] of 50 pioneers of new products found that those in lower tech markets such as packaged goods makers—Hershey, Coca-Cola, Campbell Soup, Nabisco, Procter & Gamble, Anheuser Busch, Scott tissue—had much better track records in maintaining their leading brand/market positions over time, than high-tech new product companies, such as Xerox, Sharp, Magnavox, Panasonic, Sony, Bell Labs, RCA/Thomson, Kodak, Ampex, and General Electric (whose initial lead positions often gave way to later entrants in the market). One strategic approach to this problem is to develop multiple technologies simultaneously. Motorola does this in wireless communications, betting on cellular, pager, and mobile integrated radio service—all technologies that meet similar communications needs.

Clearly, one conclusion from the study is that product leadership in high-tech markets requires a continuous commitment to integrating successive generations of technological innovation into existing, base products. Not doing so risks displacement by a competitor prepared to commit the resources needed to gain and maintain market/technology leadership.

New Product Idea Sources

Since new products can be such a vital source of growth and profitability, it clearly pays for firms to encourage a wide search for new product ideas. Otherwise, a firm may become too dependent on a few products or idea sources for its vitality. For instance, in 1992, Glaxo Holdings PLC of the U.K. earned 35 percent of its $8 billion in sales and one third of its profits (1993) from one drug—Zantac, the world's leading drug for treating stomach ulcers. Glaxo has been quite vulnerable due to such dependence on this product, which has been the company's "cash cow" for ten years.

There are many excellent sources for new product ideas. The first is, obviously, a firm's current users/customers. For instance, Reynolds Metals Co. has sold aluminum to automakers for wheels, radiators, and engine blocks. These automakers are assisting Reynolds in adapting aluminum into frames, transmissions, and auto brake parts to replace heavier (and, therefore, less fuel efficient) steel parts. In a very different market, 3M's dental customers' concerns about AIDS were the source of its idea for a dental mask to provide protection from fluids.

As mentioned previously in another context, customer complaints—often considered a source of trouble—can be a great source of new product ideas. For instance, Warner Lambert received 800-number suggestions to develop its Efferdent denture cleanser into a product to remove tough toilet bowl stains, which it has done. Many improvements in hotel services have come from comment cards completed by irate guests, including suggestions for more nonsmoking floors, hair dryers in bathrooms, lock-out mechanisms for pay television "blue movies," and emergency sewing kits for guests.

A second source for new product ideas can be a firm's distribution channels. Rubbermaid's newest children's lunch box came from an idea advanced by one of its largest retail accounts—Canadian Tire, a giant in Canadian automotive and hardware retailing. In a very different area of retailing, TopCo Inc., a retail co-op, approached the Liggett Group Inc., the smallest of America's six big U.S. tobacco firms with the idea of making generic branded cigarettes for its markets.

A third source of new product ideas is a firm's suppliers. The ideas that led to the development of "Simplesse," NutraSweet's new fat substitute, have mostly come from its connections as a supplier to a variety of food processors.

A fourth source of new products can be the firm's own employees, whether in the laboratory, in the field, or in management. 3M's Post-It notes came from its own labs, while Fred Smith, CEO of Federal Express, conceived of the idea of overnight courier delivery at a time when the world didn't appear to be especially interested in overnight delivery.

Marketing: The Key to Category Creation

Everything discussed thus far has involved marketing, but it has related almost exclusively to product development. While a unique and compelling new product concept can often create a new product category, sales often don't really take off until the product's marketing is truly polished. For example, despite Philips Electronics' prowess at inventing new product categories—the VCR, and audio compact disc, for instance—its lack of marketing agility in consumer electronics has denied it the winning market share for its products.

Consider the new product category of motion sensor lighting for outdoor applications. When introduced, motion sensor products had three immediate appeals: they were great for security (alerting homeowners when someone was approaching); they saved energy because they did not turn on unless activated by the sensor and then also turned themselves off; and lastly, they were not too difficult for an avid do-it-yourselfer to install. But the category never caught on as a mass appeal item until it was better marketed. Prices were lowered from $90 a unit to $20 or less. New decorative package design was added to increase eye appeal in stores. The installation was made "goof-proof" by reducing the number of multiple wire hook-ups and by using pre-assembled, color-coded wiring that improved ease of assembly. The result of these changes has led to more mass acceptance, and exponential category growth for outdoor lighting suppliers.

Category Clout via Product Add-Ons

In addition to more professional marketing assisting a firm in new category expansion, another tactic for growth involves exploding a category with add-on products. Dell Computer of Austin, Texas, won its initial success by using direct marketing to sell its own personal computers. But since then, it has expanded (or exploded) its offerings to include the telemarketing of 650 software programs, printers, work stations, modems, and other computer peripherals. Customers who call Dell (up to 20,000 per day) can now get one-stop shopping in addition to a computer and after-sales start-up support. More than half of Dell's sales and profits ($1.3 billion and $70 million respectively) now come from these system add-ons.

Ecko Group of Nashua, New Hampshire, dominates the bakeware and kitchen gadgets market with its extensive lines of these products. In 1991, Kmart made Ecko its sole supplier of bakeware, following a retailing trend of cutting costs by reducing the number of suppliers and relying on a single, presumably best, source. Broderbund Software of Novato, California, was largely responsible for the creation of entertaining educational software for kids aged four to twelve. Its Carmen Santiego series sold 3 million copies between 1985 and 1993; and spin-offs include a daily game show on PBS, and a line of merchandise including T-shirts and school supplies. Broderbund has even developed a CD-ROM version in foreign languages for non-English speaking markets, complete with music native to the market targeted. All of these

The Growth Masters—Creating New Categories

Company	*Product*	*Market*
Chrysler	Automobiles	Consumer
Pella	Windows	Consumer/Business
Kellogg	Food	Consumer
Gillette	Personal Care	Consumer
Prince Mfg.	Recreation	Consumer
Wilson	Recreation	Consumer
Fuji	Cameras	Consumer
Swatch	Watches	Consumer
Karsten	Recreation	Consumer/Business
Citicorp	Financial Service	Consumer
Harley-Davidson	Motorcycle	Consumer
Dell	Computers	Consumer/Business
Ecko	Housewares	Consumer
GTE	Communications	Consumer/Business
Toys R Us	Retail-Children	Consumer

add-ons have grown Broderbund's sales to $106 million (1993) with a three-year average sales growth rate of 25 percent and a profit level of $17 million.[4]

Four Steps to Product Innovation

GTE envisions a four-stage model of market sensitivity:

1. *Conformance to customer needs,* which then progresses to
2. *Customer responsiveness* (the ability to not just conform to needs but to answer customer expectations, satisfaction and specific customer group priorities) and then to
3. *Market responsiveness,* in which the company begins to customize its marketing to all segments faster and better than rivals; and lastly to

4. *Market leadership,* the ability to achieve such outstanding marketing differentiation that GTE becomes the industry, market, and customer pace-setter (i.e., the standard-setter for future desired new products in the market).

GTE believes that superior business results (sales, profits, ROI) are tied to reaching Stage 4 in any market it serves. Exhibit 1–2 illustrates these stages in market sensitivity.

The Importance of Productivity

While new products or services provide a fertile source of growth, growth in top-line revenues, it is a hollow victory indeed if profits slide.

Productivity is a must to maintain sustainable quality growth with any new product or service concept. Consider the case of Toys R Us. In 1983, sales were $1.04 billion with a $64 million profit. By 1992, sales had reached $6.1 billion, and net earnings were $340 million (combined totals of Toys R Us and Kids R Us stores). So while sales grew almost six times, so did earnings grow. How was this achieved? By close attention to the productivity of its marketing and asset management. In 1983, it took $157 million in working capital to manage its 144 stores, but a decade later, in 1992, it took only $333 million for 812 stores, a reduction in working capital per store of slightly more than $1 million to less than $400,000. Toys R Us has achieved this quality growth (sales with excellent earnings) by applying high technology in its operations. It invests heavily in state-of-the-art distribution centers, improved systems to manage its merchandise flow from suppliers to stores, and satellite technology to link its U.S. stores to its databases and via business television, all giving the company the ability to customize its merchandising mix sales by region.

Contrast this with Volkswagen, whose market share in Europe increased a full percentage point to 17.6 percent, but which is losing money despite sales growth. Its factory at Wolfsburg is using outdated technology and as a result must run almost full out, at 96 percent of

Exhibit 1–2
GTE's Four Stages in Market Sensitivity

STAGE 1 Customer Conformance
Basic competence "to do things right in the customer's eyes" is built up inside the company; i.e., pursuing organizational capabilities to provide basic quality deliverables.

↓

STAGE 2 Customer Responsiveness
The organization can understand customer's *individual* (vs. basic) expectations, satisfiers and priorities.

↓

STAGE 3 Market Responsiveness
The organization moves from being able to respond to individual customers to seeking out and capturing whole markets based on higher speed and capabilities than competitors have.

↓

STAGE 4 Market Leadership
The organization coordinates all its efforts across all its functions to consistently exceed most market requirements, and it sets the trends in the markets it is in, while leading the market throughout the various products life cycles.

capacity, to make a profit. The factory uses old methods of parts sourcing, such as in-house production which has limited its flexibility and ability to cut costs. Volkswagen is selling more cars, but showing no quality growth due to its productivity problems.[5]

Process Innovation

Significant product or service innovation often occurs only after process breakthroughs have happened, and many times the one is contingent on the other. For example, developments in automobiles owe much to Henry Ford's process breakthrough—the invention of the moving assembly line. Also, only the process of refrigeration for ice making allowed the invention of freezers and home-based, low-cost refrigerators. In addition, George Eastman's invention of celluloid film production led to all sorts of product inventions, up to and including 35mm cameras and mass production of film rolls.

This concept of innovation is so pervasive that it deserves at least one more extended example. When Alistair Pilkington figured out a way to make flat glass in one continuous process (as opposed to five separate processes of mixing, melting, casting, annealing, and grinding/polishing), it allowed glass makers to automate with enormous efficiency gains from a formally labor-intensive manufacturing set-up. In addition, firms making glass could concentrate on glass properties, shapes, and strengths rather than just making the glass economically (labor costs reduced by 80 percent and energy costs reduced by 50 percent). This process breakthrough in the early 1950s single-handedly produced thousands of new types of glass for autos, trucks, office skyscrapers, store fronts, rapid transit, with new properties, shapes, strengths, and thermal efficiencies.

Process innovations always facilitate product innovations, but these often occur in waves. For instance, photography has moved from daguerreotype, to tin process, to glass plate developing, dry plates, celluloid roll film and, today, electronic imaging. Each successive wave of process innovation creates new products, but often the same firm does not develop each successive wave of innovation. General Electric moved easily from incandescent lamp manufacturing to vacuum tubes for radios and television because each shared common processes. But G.E. did not invent transistors, the process technology that later revolutionized radios and television. Similarly, it was Polaroid, not Kodak, that introduced instant photography. So leadership in process innovation often shifts between firms just as market share does between business rivals. However, if process breakthroughs are critical to a firm's ongoing success, it is crucial for them to adopt them even if they are the inventor. As PC's replaced typewriters, IBM recognized the need to migrate to the new technology even though Apple invented it. Similarly, no tire maker could exist today without radial tires even though the radial tire manufacturing process was spearheaded by Michelin in Europe. Initially, Goodyear and Firestone saw the new process as harmful to their enormously successful and profitable bias and belted businesses.

Process breakthroughs are as key to service businesses as they are to product manufacturing. The hub-and-spoke system of airline routing helped lead Federal Express's success in overnight courier package delivery in the U.S. New information technology breakthroughs in banking allowed for automated teller machines, debit cards, telebanking, cash management accounts, and many other financial instruments considered commonplace today.

Customization: The New Product Frontier

While category dominance of the type Toys R Us exhibits (it sells 40 percent of all U.S. toys sold) is key, there are two other important variants on new product sales. The most innovative and, recently, the most discussed is customization (or "mass customization"), the process of tailoring the new product or service specifically to the individual customer's requirements. Customization can be as simple as altering automated teller machines so that they can be used by Spanish-speaking individuals, or as complex as producing a separate product for an individual account as does Flexcon of Spencer, Massachusetts. Flexcon, unlike most giant chemical companies that provide multipurpose generic adhesives to printers (for printed packaging materials), develops a special formula for each printer's needs. Its production formula is so versatile that it can supply custom-tailored orders of one-tenth the size offered by its competitors.

As markets fragment, customers demand and often get customized products. For instance:

- Ping, using a golfer's glove size, height, and fingertip-to-floor measurements will make irons appropriate to the player's needed grip, shaft length, and club lies (resting position on the ground).
- S.C. Johnson and Sons customizes its Raid insect spray by 18 different U.S. regions, so that its sprays can target the worst pests in each area (e.g., fleas in Birmingham and Tampa; cockroaches in New York and Houston).
- Bata, the world's top shoe producer, manufactures its shoes in one hundred factories located in different locations around the world to turn out shoes tailored to the demands of local markets.
- Nestlé blends different coffees for the British than the French, because the British like it with milk while the French drink it black. Similarly, to a Canadian, a "regular" coffee means with cream and sugar, while a "regular" coffee to an Italian is black. So the taste of Nestlé's coffee and even its advertising vary by market.
- Northern Telecom makes its telecommunications products so that they fit local market differences in electrical voltages and varying standards for phone jacks.
- Mattel's sales of Barbie dolls in Japan succeeded only when the doll's physical characteristics were adjusted to reflect the culture.

The Strengths of Customization

Smart customization strategies can often greatly increase a firm's market share and growth. For instance, in the U.S. truck-trailer manufacturing business, total industry sales have fallen from 214,300 units in 1988 to 140,500 units in 1992, a huge decline. This overall industry decline has knocked back the market leaders, Fruehauf, Great Dane, and Strick, by huge percentages (64 percent for Fruehauf and 25 percent each for Great Dane and Strick since 1988). Yet one firm bucking this trend is Wabash National, whose 1992 sales were $300 million, up from $191 million in 1991. A new firm, Wabash National grew its share of market from 3.1 percent in 1991 to 10.1 percent in 1992—all from a new firm not even in existence in 1983.

How did Wabash accomplish this growth in a declining industry? It produces 100 trailers per day, each approximately 7.5 tons, each with 5,000 parts—and customizes them by order. The company makes these custom trailers for a wide variety of clients with very different needs. For example, for Federal Express, it makes trailers with rollers built into floors for faster shipping and container loading. It manufactures special custom trailers for Libby Owens Ford to transport glass in deep wells built into the trailers. Wabash even makes low slung "axle-less" trailers, with each wheel independently suspended, for Walt Disney Company to transport laundry and other products in its low-clearance underground tunnels at Disney World. Wabash customizes Mayflower's units to hold an entire household's furniture.[6] Wabash's ability to turn its production lines loose, even on very small job lots, has allowed it to command a 5 percent price premium over competitors who cannot add custom features.

Although it's in a less "mobile" industry, Fluor, one of the world's global engineering and construction giants, does the same thing. It customizes its services to all worldwide clients whether it is engineering power plants, coal and energy operations, oil or chemical facilities, or

The Growth Masters—Customization

Company	***Product***	***Market***
Flexcon	Chemicals	Business
Ping	Recreation	Consumer/Business
S.C. Johnson	Household Products	Consumer
Bata	Footwear	Consumer
Nestlé	Food	Consumer
Northern Telecom	Telecommunications	Consumer/Business
Wabash National	Truck-trailer manufacturing	Business
Fluor	Engineering/Construction	Business
Motorola	Wireless Communications	Consumer/Business

process facilities for lead-recycling, pharmaceuticals, pulp and paper, or other industrial operations. As a result, its revenues have grown from \$3.9 billion in 1987 to \$6.7 billion in 1991, and net earnings for that same period grew even more impressively—from \$27 million to \$161 million. Fluor has deliberately diversified its customer base while customizing its approach to new markets. Fluor only goes after projects in industries in which it can effectively apply its superior project execution skills to customized projects. Successful customization has placed Fluor in the top 25 percent of Fortune 500 U.S. companies for much of the 1980s and 1990s.

Using the same principle, Motorola has greatly expanded its pager business by customizing the product by user or type. For example, in mainland China it markets a particular model that is attractive—that is, affordable, portable, and unobtrusive—to working mothers of young children. The pager enables the women to keep in contact with babysitters. Such customization and the imaginative thinking that goes with it have helped Motorola capture an 85 percent global market share in pagers.

Portfolios of Products: All in the Family

Portfolio expansion strategies involve marketing "good, better, best" versions of a new products so that all of the market segment's price-value sensitivities are covered.

Portfolio expansion has, of course, been practiced by packaged goods makers and auto manufacturers for many years. Nestlé has coffee products in the premium, middle, and lower cost spectrums of the instant coffee market. Ford and others cater to all tastes by model proliferation in subcompacts, compacts, mid-size, full-size, and luxury automobiles.

This "good, better, best" strategy is practiced in industrial markets as well. For instance, 3M sells more than 400 constructions of tapes, suiting different needs, price-points, and types of customers, such as it sells low-end utility masking tapes, medium grades, and high-performance masking tapes used in painting applications that must withstand the high temperatures of automotive paint ovens.

Naming the Family Members

The expanded portfolio strategy of "good, better, best" offerings works best when a firm can create a family brand and then add to its family.

Sanford Company, in Bellwood, Illinois, consistently produces a 24 percent return on equity and sales increases of 14 percent year after year by producing a family of pens, pencils and markers for doing everything from marking clothes in laundromats to making no-smear notes on fax paper. The company produces colored markers for toddlers of all ages and talents. Broderbund, discussed earlier in this chapter, markets one software program, waits to see if it's a success, and then adds to the family. Its successful program "Where in the World Is Carmen Santiego?" teaches children geography. Now also in the family are "Where in Time Is Carmen Santiego?" and "Where in America's Past Is Carmen Santiego?" that teach other skills to kids. Broderbund's portfolio expansion grew 1992 sales to 75 million, up by 34 percent from 1991 and its profitability is also up 36% to 10 million on its sales.

The Growth Masters—Portfolios of Products

Company	***Product***	***Market***
Sanford	Pens/Markers	Consumer/Business
Broderbund	Entertainment/Education	Consumer
3M	Office Supplies	Consumer/Business
Molex	Electronics	Business
Renishaw PLC	Measurement Instruments	Business

3M has launched more than 100 variations of its Post-It brand notes since the first offering, so that its family now includes notes of different sizes, shapes, colors, lined versus unlined, with messages or blank, in different thicknesses and some for specific uses such as fax notes or Post-It Tape Flags for indexing. So successful has this portfolio expansion strategy been that its primary competitor Avery withdrew from the market in the face of 3M's blizzard of new product offshoots.

Nike and Reebok both use a portfolio expansion strategy each time they introduce a new line of sport- or activity-specific athletic shoes, whether for basketball, jogging, tennis, or aerobics. Branding the Nike or Reebok name and logo across any new family entries maintains the family look of the products.

Protecting New Products

A new product created through one of the strategies discussed in this chapter may or may not create growth, but one thing is certain: a successful new product—one that creates quality growth—will create competition in the form of products that attempt to improve on an innovation or attempt to imitate a product benefit. In fact, in a great many markets, protecting new products through patent protection is vitally important. Consider the case of Renishaw PLC, whose 70 percent market share dominates the field of "metrology," the science of very precisely measuring machined parts, using probes calibrated to within

Case 2

Molex, Inc.: Growing by New Products, Customization, and an Expanded Portfolio of Products

One would be very hard-pressed to find a more salient example of sustainable quality growth via new products and their variants than that of Molex Inc., of Lisle, Illinois.

Molex's financial results show consistent, sustained growth in sales, gross profit, and net income that has fueled its earnings per share each year since 1983. See Exhibit 1–3.

New Products

Molex has achieved its growth through a continuous stream of new products in the electrical, electronic, and fiber optic interconnect market. In 1992 alone it introduced 150 new products and secured 140 new patents. Its product lines include 40,000 products, more than half of which are less than five years old.

One-Stop Shopping—Expanded Product Portfolios

While the overall market for connectors grew only 1.9 percent in 1991–92, Molex's sales grew 8.5 percent, mostly because, through product proliferation, it positioned itself as the single source for all of its customers' interconnector needs. For instance, as new product categories, such as fiber optic connectors or memory card interconnection, emerge in the market, Molex has pioneered the categories, with good, better, best offerings to suit industries as diverse as computers, laser printers, photocopiers, home entertainment, and even "smart home" systems (the infrastructure to automate a residential house's telephones, audio/video signal distribution, energy use, lighting, and security controls).

Customization

Molex product designers work intimately with the staff engineers of such companies as Sony, Philips, IBM, AT&T, Ford, Kodak, Canon and Haworth to customize connectors for specific customers' needs. Molex accomplishes this with local and global design facilities in 48 manufacturing facilities strategically located in 20 nations on five continents. Molex's customization strategy has worked so well that 74 percent of its sales are outside the USA and it holds a leading position in the connector market in Japan and throughout Asia (representing one-half of Molex's 1992 sales and profits).

(Continued on next page)

Exhibit 1–3
Molex, Inc., Financial Performance (millions)

	Sales	Gross Profit	Net Income	Earnings per Share
1992	$776.1	$318.3	$67.5	$1.35
1991	$707.9	$297.9	$64.6	$1.30
1990	$594.3	$256.6	$62.0	$1.24
1989	$571.8	$257.1	$57.7	$1.14
1988	$502.3	$240.0	$59.2	$1.17
1987	$386.7	$174.8	$43.4	$ .86
1986	$291.9	$133.5	$32.0	$ .64
1985	$253.2	$120.3	$30.9	$ .61
1984	$252.2	$132.5	$38.2	$ .77
1983	$175.9	$ 88.7	$22.0	$ .44

Source: Selected figures from Ten-Year Financial Summary; Molex, Inc., Annual Report.

five thousandths of an inch (.005 inches). Renishaw's invention of a ruby-tipped probe fitted to a computer allows precise, often three-dimensional, measurements for everything from machine tools to car engines and most watch parts. General Motor's Saturn auto plant has 24 Renishaw probes, while NASA uses the probes to accurately fit heat shield tiles in place on the space shuttle.

Renishaw's device, invented in the mid-seventies, was duplicated through patent infringement by GTE–Valeron in the early eighties. Renishaw defended the patent at a cost of $1 million and as a result gained a settlement of more than $10 million and a blanket prohibition against GTE–Valeron ever producing or even servicing its existing copy-cat versions. Renishaw's sales and profits have grown since 1983 from $13 million and $32 million respectively in 1991. It has defended its patent in 12 suits against Carl Zeiss in Germany and against 21 Japanese rivals, all successfully.[7]

Summary

Future chapters will delineate other platforms for growth, but as Molex and the many other examples in this chapter illustrate, the basics of good business are alive and well. The kind of imagination and innovative spirit that create entirely new kinds of products and change the essential ways we live, work, and conduct our affairs is still a catalyst to growth. So too is the spirit of customer service reflected in the newest approach to new products—customization that comes from listening to and anticipating customers' needs. And portfolio expansion, the ability to build on one's initial success, is still a sound approach to quality growth.

Notes

1. For an interview with the founder of SMH, Nicolas Hayek, see the *Harvard Business Review,* Mar./April 1993: 99–110: "Message and Muscle: An Interview with Swatch Titan Nicolas Hayek," by William Taylor.

2. Michael Czinkota and Masaaki Kotabe, "Product Development the Japanese Way," *Journal of Business Strategy,* Nov./Dec. 1990: 31–36.
3. Marketing Science Institute, Working Paper Series Report #92–124, Sept. 1992: "Do Pioneers Really Have Long-Term Advantages? A Historical Analysis," by Peter Golder and Gerard Tellis, Cambridge, Mass.
4. Andrew Kapfer, "Broderbund—Identify a Need, Turn a Profit," *Fortune,* Nov. 30, 1992: 78–79. See also *Forbes,* "The Best Small Companies in America," Nov. 7, 1994, p. 242.
5. John Templeman (in Geneva) and Gail E. Shares (in Bonn), "A Hard U-Turn at Volkswagen," *Business Week,* Mar. 15, 1993: 47.
6. Edward O. Welles, "Least Likely to Succeed," *Inc.* Magazine, Dec. 1992: 74–86.
7. Jeff Ferry, "The Wotton World Beater," *Management Today* (U.K.), March 1992: 62–63; and Peter Fuhrman, "The Reluctant Entrepreneur," *Forbes,* Feb. 15, 1993: 75–76. Both articles detail Renishaw PLC's corporate growth and success due to its patents.

Chapter 2

Growing Your Business Through New Markets

New Users, New Uses, and New Places

> Have you ever been sunburned on a cloudy day? Like the sun, change can burn you even when you can't see it. Organizations are in danger when they accommodate gradually heightening dysfunction. Eventually the best of change grows great enough to hurt them.
>
> **Daryl R. Conner**
> *Managing at the Speed of Change*

Companies that rest on their laurels are headed for disaster. Every company must continue to follow and respond to the basics of its markets—its products' users (its customers), its products' uses (its customers' needs), and their locations ("where they are" both physically and psychologically). The company that tracks these accurately will never be caught short by its markets or by shrewd competitors. Those that do not find new uses for their products and services, entice new users into their markets, or expand to new locales where customers are unserved or underserved will eventually get burned. As the above quotation so eloquently states, accommodating dysfunction can lead to a firm's demise, especially in regard to slowed growth in the company's user or usage customer base. Each of these three strategies for refreshing the firm's growth—finding new users, finding new uses and finding new locations—are powerful antidotes to the dysfunctionality described above.

Johnson Electric Holding, Inc., has moved on all three of these strategies to become the fastest growing, most profitable firm in the global manufacturing of micromotors. Begun in 1959 as a maker of micromotors for toys, it reached out in the 1970s to new users such as Black and Decker, Sunbeam, Kodak, and Moulinex. Its motors' uses expanded to new uses in applications such as controlling power door locks or seat adjustments in cars, as well as cordless tool usage. Lastly, it sought overseas markets from its base in Hong Kong, so that today its micromotors go to Japan, Europe and North America, instead of only to local Hong Kong's toy and small appliance makers.

Growing the Firm's Base of Users

Seeking out and finding new users for a company's products is a surefire recipe for growth. Cosmetics makers used to define their target market as women until they reframed their growth potential to include men. Today, men's cosmetics is a significant segment, approximately 20 to 25 percent of the market size for female cosmetics.

Bata Shoe went to Africa to convert non-shoe-wearing peoples to wearing shoes and as a result has become one of the world's largest shoe manufacturers. Honda convinced middle-class men that riding a motorcycle wasn't confined to young leather-jacketed men with a penchant for the machismo—and a new market segment opened up to them.

In July 1992, Gerber, the U.S. leader in baby foods, launched a whole new line of 23 products aimed at a class of non-users, toddlers aged one to three. Called the Graduates Line, it includes enriched juices, microwavable dishes, diced vegetables, and finger foods. Gerber hoped to supplant parents' current custom of feeding toddlers their own prepared table foods. To address these influencers—the parents—Gerber has fortified all its dishes with protein, iron, and calcium while controlling salt and sugar content to lower levels than found in most adult table foods. The company extensively sampled its new toddlers' line at nursery schools and at parenting fairs. Gerber hoped to duplicate the diaper manufacturers' success in targeting older babies with diapers specifically designed for their needs. The Gerber campaign launch was the largest in the company's history, and sales of its Graduates line rose to $47 million, or 6.2 percent, of the total 1993 baby food market—only 18 months after product launch.

Finding New Users

There often are unlimited ways to target new users unfamiliar with a company's products.

Consider the lowly flashlight. In 1992 retail sales of flashlights topped $340 million from such large, successful marketers as Duracell U.S.A., Rayovac, Eveready Battery, Lumilite Products, and Garrity Industries. The vast majority of flashlights were targeted to male customers, but now—with jazzy packaging, "softer" designs, and value/gift pack type pricing—manufacturers have begun selling more flashlights to women.

Why? Because more households are headed by single or divorced women, a changing demographic that has required these firms to rethink their flashlight designs and marketing. New designs are lighter and made better to fit a woman's smaller hand. They are easier to take apart and reassemble and have more decorative colors. In addition to the traditional outlets, such as hardware, automotive and do-it-yourself lumber centers, these flashlights are being marketed more in retail channels, such as grocery stores, discount stores, and drug chains, where women are more apt to buy them.

Complementary Products

Growing with new users often requires the help of complementary products, especially in the case of such volatile categories as electronic, telecommunications, and entertainment products. For example, film users grow as camera placements grow, and this same phenomenon exists for videocassette recorders, camcorders, and videotape; computers and diskettes; cellular phones and air time sales; and so forth. The implication for marketers seeking to grow new users in these types of markets should be clear: assist the hardware or complementary product marketer's efforts in order to gain the pull-through effects for their own products. For example, manufacturers of bar code labels would do well to assist bar code scanner manufacturers to increase their scanner placements.

Sometimes, of course, a firm decides to make "the razor and the blades," such as Sony in the video business, Kodak in cameras and film, but in many other instances, the potential for such integration does not exist on a practical level—as in the case of Microsoft, which makes software but not hardware, and 3M, which makes videotape but not VCRs or camcorders.

New Forms of Competition

As new users appear, the dynamics of competition often change. For example, the growth of the "Quality Movement" has brought new competition for management consultants helping companies implement Total Quality Management (TQM) systems. Some specialist firms, such as Crosby and Associates, are dedicated to the TQM market exclusively. Yet as the number of new users (i.e., more companies seeking to implement quality programs) has increased, two other types of competitive consultants have appeared—traditional management consulting arms of the national accounting firms, such as Price Waterhouse, Arthur Andersen Consulting, or Coopers and Lybrand, and training firms, such as Achieve Corporation, which has always provided training services and simply added Total Quality Management training to its portfolio of services. Traditional book and magazine publishers faced entirely new competitors when Apple Computer helped pioneer desktop publishing, allowing individuals or small firms to economically self-publish their own newsletters, books, and journals and sell them into the same markets as traditional publishers.

Needed: Unconventional Thinking

Just as Bata Shoe sold shoes to people who previously had gone barefoot, a company ferreting out new users often needs an unconventional and new version of possible users. Consider Nestlé, the world leader in instant coffee, condensed milk, frozen food, baby food, and mineral water. (Nestlé owns Carnation and Perrier.) Since its goal is to double sales from $36 billion to $72 billion within 10 years, it must find new users for its products. Nestlé cannot possibly reach its goal through new products or acquisitions alone.

So what is the company doing? It is trying to convince the people of the world's largest *tea* drinking nation—China—to drink *coffee.* It wants noncustomers to become its brand's users. To solidify its push, Nestlé is now manufacturing both Nestlé coffee and Coffee-Mate creamer inside China. The plans to convert the Chinese to coffee are firm, and Nestlé is off to a good start, with sales growing in this region at 13 percent per year compared to a total growth rate in the rest of the developed world of only 1 to 2 percent.[1] Its share of market is still far below 2 percent overall, so the company has plenty of room to grow.

Nestlé is betting that once the Chinese show themselves open to new tastes and Western-style food products, there will be markets for a variety of other products (which the company is also starting to manufacture in South-East Asia), such as ice cream, frozen Cantonese-style dinners, infant formula, and even chocolate products.

In Search of a Better Product

Revitalizing growth with non-users doesn't have to mean looking far afield from the current user profile. Sometimes growth is possible simply by delivering an existing product in a new way. Consider Elan PLC in Athlone, Ireland, whose 1992 sales grew to $10 million, up 52 percent from 1991. Elan specializes in delivering proven drugs in new ways that help revitalize sales and gain new users for otherwise mature products. For instance, Elan has technologies that allow for timed-released drug formulations that are either taken orally (by mouth) or absorbed transdermally (through the skin). By applying these technologies to drugs, such as Lederle (Verelen's drug) or Marion Merrell

Dow's Cardizem (both hypertensive drugs that originally had to be taken orally four times per day), it has grown its sales very quickly. Its timed-released technology allows patients to take a drug once-a-day, greatly increasing the number of sales to non-users. (Doctors prescribe these kinds of drug formulations to certain patients who have problems with the traditional four-times-per-day dosages for these drugs). Elan earns a royalty on sales of all drugs that incorporate its technology.

Sometimes simply satisfying a market differently generates new users. The high-stress world of the business traveler provides a case in point. The Hyatt hotel chain is growing its user base by doing the best job in the hotel industry at managing airport-based hotels—the one place where all business travelers are sure to be at one time or another. Its Air Hyatt is the best package of special perks and services in the industry, with the result that its airport hotels are increasing their occupancy rates faster than rivals. As a segment the "stressed traveler market" has grown to over $4.5 billion from next to nothing 10 years ago.

The Growth Masters—New Users

Company	*Product*	*Market*
Johnson Electric Holding	Micromotors	Business
Bata Shoe Mfg.	Shoes	Consumer
Gerber	Food-Children	Consumer
Nestlé	Food	Consumer
Elan PLC	Pharmaceuticals	Business
Hyatt	Hotels	Business
Safety-Kleen	Industrial Solvents/Recycling	Business

Case 3

The Classic Case of Finding New Users: Safety-Kleen Company

Founded in 1968, Safety-Kleen Company of Chicago, Illinois, represents an ideal example of a firm with a voracious appetite for new users. In its early years the company grew to 275 outlets that provided equipment and solvent for cleaning small parts used by car dealerships, service stations, truck fleets, and auto repair shops in the normal course of their business. It then expanded its services to include replacement of contaminated solvents with virgin solvent and recycling and reclaiming of dirty solvent.

This relatively small service business—its first-year sales were $1.2 million in 1969, with losses of $400,000 in the process—grew rapidly by winning new business (converting non-user shops) to its service network. By 1981 it had grown to $134.8 million in sales, earning $10 million in profit and returning shareholders 29 percent on their equity invested.

In 1980, Safety-Kleen began to look for new users of its hazardous fluid-handling and recycling/reclaiming capabilities and found them in two very different industries: dry cleaning shops and metal working/metal finishing and electronics industries, both of which use large volumes of cleaning or degreasing fluids in manufacturing. Safety-Kleen offered both of these non-users a variety of testing, transportation, and waste-processing services.

In 1987, Safety-Kleen once again targeted non-users, this time in general industry, by selling applications of its core technology, its cleaning and fluid recovery system services. This move alone boosted its user base by 110,000 accounts during 1991. At the same time the company applied its core capability of recycling and transporting to other non-users—businesses with used oil requiring recovery. It opened 108 branches to recycle used oil and to process oil from used oil filters from its existing auto and industrial customers. Safety-Kleen re-refines the used oil and resells it to oil companies, which blend in new additives. In 1991, it recovered more than 108 million gallons from this base of customers.

Safety-Kleen's efforts to find new users for its services have grown its user base to 500,000 companies, including firms in Europe, and led to a much stronger and more diversified portfolio of businesses. Safety-Kleen's financial diversification and results are shown on Exhibit 2–1. As these outstanding results demonstrate, seeking out non-users for services or products can grow a firm's business for many years at average growth rates far in excess of general economic indicators such as industrial production or GNP.

Figure 2–1
Safety-Kleen's Sales, Profits, and Business Portfolio (millions)

Historical Growth

	Sales	Profits
1991	$ 695.0	$ 51.5
1986	$ 255.3	$ 28.2
1981	$ 134.8	—
1976	$ 47.4	$ 2.7
1971	$ 7.5	$ 353.0
1969	$ 1.1	$ (400.0)

1991 Growth Sectors

Business Portfolio	1991 yr sales	1991 per yr growth
Automotive Repair	$235.6	4%
Industrial Services	163.9	34%
Used Oil Recovery	95.5	16%
Dry Cleaning, Paint Recovery	141.4	10%
Total		
North America	$636.4	
Europe	58.4	100%
	$695.0	18%

Source: All data are from the 1991 Safety-Kleen Co. Annual Report to Shareholders.

Growth via New Uses

Just as new users can provide a firm with an engine of growth, so too can finding new uses for a firm's products. For instance, Church and Dwight, makers of Arm & Hammer Baking Soda, grew sales of its base product from $127 million in 1981 to $485 million a decade later by extending its uses. This simple product is now used for lead prevention in municipal water supplies, as an air freshener, a carpet deodorizer, a toothpaste, a laundry detergent, a toxic-emission reducer in gas power plants, a silverware cleaner and even as a sand-blasting additive that is safer for users' lungs. Similarly, the aluminum producers Reynolds Metals and Alcoa have done an outstanding job of developing the uses for aluminum including: grain bins, baseball bats, siding, windows, doors, boats, roofing, appliance parts, beverage cans, and automobile parts.[2]

DuPont has done a similarly marvelous job of finding expanded uses for lycra, nylon, kevlar, and other fibers it produces. Lycra, its superstretch polymer, is now used in jazzy new clothing, a long way from its first use in girdles in 1959 and, later, in stretch swimsuits. Similarly, Loctite, one of the world's largest, fastest-growing adhesives firms, owes much of its growth to new uses for its broad range of anaerobic adhesives.

Product Variations

Sometimes a product can be used as-is or nearly so for a new use of application no one had thought of before. But often finding new uses for a firm's products or services means some imaginative product re-engineering. Sony's Sports Walkman gave its popular product a big jolt of new growth from its use during jogging, walking or work-out sessions at the gym, but that didn't happen by accident. The Sports Walkman was re-engineered in terms of contemporary colors, more robust construction, and operational simplicity, features that were specifically built into the product for this different use. Analogously, the home market for photocopiers developed once the larger office models were made compact enough to sit on a desktop.

Today's multipurpose technologies often allow for the spin-off of multiple product variations at affordable production costs, and this logic applies to service organizations as well. For instance, by reconfiguring its restaurants into multiple formats and sizes, McDonald's has been able to enter new-use locations such as stadiums, universities, airports, military bases, and other nontraditional outlets. Similarly, when 3M added neon and dramatic colors to its synthetic casting material for medical uses, it got far greater usage of casting by doctors treating kids with broken limbs, who responded to the "neat" colors. The redesign of automated teller machines to add more features than pure cash withdrawal, such as bill payments and account transfers, has resulted in expanded usage and more service revenue for financial services institutions.

Continental Consumer Products, of Birmingham, Michigan, has expanded usage of hydrogen peroxide and isopropyl alcohol, products sold in the first aid section of drug stores. Continental has developed gel formats of these products, packaged in one-ounce tubes, which makes the product more easily storable, more transportable, and more economical to use because the buyer can purchase smaller quantities of these antiseptics, which are often used only occasionally (and often only for a one-time purpose).

The Importance of "Fresh" Marketing Approaches

Rethinking uses sometimes requires a complete overhaul of many marketing tactics, from advertising and promotion to packaging and product ingredients. L & F Products, the company that makes Lysol, saw sales slipping and decided to expand the brand's market positioning to include use as a disinfectant for killing germs that cause colds and the flu (rotovirus and rhinovirus) in daycare and other institutional care settings.

The company launched a massive television campaign and a public relations blitz to try and move Lysol usage outside the bathroom to these kinds of facilities. L & F updated Lysol's packaging graphics, set up an Infection Control Council comprised of top doctors and healthcare specialists, and reinstated its old ad claim of being "concentrated to make 99 times more disinfecting solution." As a result of these efforts, L & F's sales are trending back up by virtue of new uses in these new markets.

Product Positioning

The microwave oven was originally positioned for cooking. That was its first, and was considered its target, use by microwave manufacturers. In fact, its most frequent use has been for heating food, a warming versus cooking function. And an even more specific new use is emerging for it—for snack preparation, as in the case of microwaveable popcorn. So popular has this latest use been that 15 percent of American homes have two microwaves, one in the kitchen and a second one often put in the den or family room for snack preparation convenience.

It is important when deciding how to grow uses to understand how customers actually use the firm's products versus "intended" uses. The original intended or anticipated use for VCRs was for taping television shows (especially movies), yet the public's main use has evolved to playing rented tapes. Thus, rather than programming their VCRs to tape network TV programs, most users are playing rented videos.

On a very different "track," Nike and Reebok originally assumed that their athletic shoes would be used to perform athletic endeavors, yet today far more of their shoes are purchased as fashion statements, and their primary use is for just walking around. 3M has repositioned a variety of medical and surgical products originally developed for humans for sale and use by veterinarians. Included are tapes, surgical incise drapes, casting materials, wraps, surgical staples, and sterilizing products.

Market Integration and Usage Growth

Sometimes markets for products are static, but more often they aren't. Customers often find new applications for products as they move between environments. As they move between home and work, they seek out products they use in one context for use in the other.

A variety of products originally intended for use in the workplace, such as fax machines and copiers, now have significant home use. For instance, 3M's Post-It Notes, so successful in office markets, have found fast-growing use in home markets. Black and Decker's drills, sanders, and other tools first caught on in professional contractor markets before gaining large-scale use by homeowners.

This same phenomenon works also in reverse: consumers discover products that industry later adapts to its uses. The industrial uses for baking soda from Arm & Hammer capitalized on its initial success in home-use markets, and VCR use for home entertainment has stimulated industrial use of VCRs as a tool for training or communicating to employees.

Market migration can also occur from very special-use markets over into more mainstream ones. 3M's sandpaper and masking tapes, originally used in specialized applications, such as automotive body painting, eventually became mass-use products. Similarly, WD-40, the all-purpose spray for lubrication or protection of metal parts, was first developed for military use to keep water from causing rust or other damage to rifles in the moist, humid jungles of Viet Nam. Military personnel returning home eventually bought the spray for their hunting rifles, and today WD-40 is used for all sorts of home applications and is a common product found in most mechanics' and do-it-yourselfers' tool boxes. WD-40's sales totaled $104 million in 1992, and new uses keep sales growth rates in the 5 to 6 percent range.

Helping Your Customer's Customer

Some products have limited market potential as products in their own right, but have enormous potential as parts or components of other products. In such cases the customer of your customer is your customer. The classic case of this "customer once removed" relationship is Monsanto's Nutra Sweet artificial sweetener. Monsanto has created huge growth for its branded artificial sweetener by helping the firms it supplies (soft drink makers, diversified food processing firms) to convince *their* customers (pop drinkers, ice cream eaters) of the superiority of the Nutra Sweet additive. Monsanto advertises cooperatively with its accounts to position the Nutra Sweet brand, label, and message with the ultimate users of its customer's products in mind. Similarly, 3M does this same thing when it works with ski wear manufacturers or outer wear companies to advertise its Thinsulate brand insulation. Using "hang-tags" on garments to communicate Thinsulate's merits to the retail coat-buying public, 3M influences its customers' customers to look for and ask for Thinsulate-lined ski jackets, top coats, and other products.

In some cases, industry-wide organizations comprised of multiple producers band together to do the same thing. For example, the Wool Council trumpets the virtues of wool garments to the general public and to manufacturers. The intent is to boost growth in the use of the ingredient or the specific brand (such as wool or Thinsulate) through

The Growth Masters—New Uses

Company	***Product***	***Market***
Church and Dwight	Baking Soda	Consumer/Business
Loctite	Anaerobic Adhesives	Business
Reynolds Metals	Aluminum	Consumer/Business
McDonald's	Food	Consumer
Continental Consumer Products	First Aid	Consumer
L & F Products	Cleaners	Consumer/Business
WD-40 Company	Lubricant	Consumer/Business
Monsanto/Nutra Sweet	Artificial Sweetener	Consumer/Business
Betz Laboratories	Engineering	Business

the power of advertising and branding. The orange growers of California created the Sunkist brand for this very reason: to convince more consumers that Sunkist (i.e., California) oranges are superior and thus to increase purchase of Sunkist oranges and, secondarily, to boost the purchase of the category in general. The creation and promotion of the Sunkist brand lifted California oranges out of the "commodity" category by conveying an image of special freshness and taste to the consumer.

Growing via New Locales

New uses and users can be anywhere, so depending on the extent of your market reach, you can find new customers in many new locales, from around the corner to around the world.

Consider the case of Blockbuster Entertainment Corp. of Fort Lauderdale, Florida. With $1.25 billion in revenues, it is the world's largest video rental chain. And much of its growth has come from overseas expansion. Blockbuster has 2,989 stores, 952 of which are in

Case 4

Growing via New Uses: Betz Laboratories

Betz Laboratories is a global Fortune 500 corporation, a world leader in engineered water and process treatment programs. Founded in 1925, the company has grown from $252 million in sales ($3.2 million in profit) in 1981 to $665 million ($16 million profit) 10 years later.

Betz produces and markets both the specialty chemicals and technical and laboratory services required for the treatment of water and wastewater as well as the processing of various types of papers, chemicals, and manufactured goods. The company prescribes the appropriate treatment for water so that its customers avoid problems of scale build-up, corrosion, and deposit formation. By monitoring and prescribing the treatment required, Betz preserves or enhances the efficiency of its customers' plant operations.

The majority of Betz's growth occurred as it expanded the usage of its systems into new fields. The company has played the "growth by application" trump card very well by having a diversified and flexible approach to customer needs. For instance, it tailors its mix of treatment programs to the countries in which it operates. So in Finland Betz finds its strongest uses in paper processing, while in Belgium it concentrates on oil-refining applications. Its technologies and markets are broad-spectrum in potential since it can provide engineered water treatment programs for large buildings, hospitals, and schools or for light industry. Its industrial process treatments find applications in paper and steel mills, hydrocarbon processing (refineries and petrochemical plants), metal-finishing industries, and power generation facilities (for treatment of boiler waters, coolant waters, close-up, and waste waters). A recent new use for its products and services has provided an unusual benefit to increased electricity production. Its chemicals are being used to remove mussel infestations, whose multiplication and growth can clog power plant systems, thereby reducing water flow needed for electricity production.

Even during the 1990–91 recession, Betz grew its sales by new uses by 12 percent over the previous year, and its net earnings increased by 15 percent. The key to the company's long-term success had been developing broad-spectrum products and services and then finding new and growing product uses that save its customers money.

9 foreign countries, and plans to add another 1,200 outside the U.S. by 1995. In Japan alone, Blockbuster, in partnership with Den Fujita (which runs McDonald's in Japan) plans to open a thousand outlets by the year 2003, many of them next to McDonald's restaurants.

By bringing professional marketing to a fragmented industry, Blockbuster is gaining momentum in Britain, Canada, Austria, Japan, Chile, Mexico, Australia, Spain, and Venezuela.[3] These markets in many cases represent even greater potential than the U.S. because video rentals per capita are extremely high in such countries as the U.K. and Chile, where television offerings are limited in variety, and many small villages/towns without cinemas predominate. Blockbuster's strategy is an excellent example of finding differences in markets where only similarities are apparent and finding similarities where only differences are obvious.

Discovering "New" Locales

Finding a new locale for your product or service doesn't necessarily mean going halfway around the world. Sometimes a new locale is right around the corner or at least in your home country. Underserved markets at home can offer inviting sales prospects. Key Corporation of Albany, New York, is a medium-sized bank that has grown ten times its 1982 size (in assets, to $32 billion) by moving into small, poorly served communities, buying up small-town banks, and injecting better management into them. Building on its expertise in serving consumers and small businesses, it has acquired banks in places such as Ashland, Maine; Big Piney, Wyoming; and Tumwater, Washington. Because there were few competitor banks, Key Corp. has been able to avoid price wars with other banks for customers.

Emphasizing good service rather than low price, Key Corp. has used state-of-the-art information technology to automate these banks, providing credit and loan information electronically from its Albany headquarters to its 850 far-flung branches, including its 20 branches in Alaska. The result has been not only tremendous growth but also a return on equity over the 1982–92 period averaging 25.8 percent better than such super regionals as Banc One and Wachovia.

Knowing How to Pick Them: Sizing Up New Markets

Entering a new market—whether a foreign market on another continent or an underserved domestic one only a stone's throw from company headquarters—requires the same basic assessment skills needed for any marketing decision. *New* is a matter of definition, and failing to understand the meaning of the term accurately can have disastrous consequences. It is vital that you understand the market structure in each geographic zone and be able to identify the forces that may act to limit an apparently good opportunity. A market that looks underserved may in fact be underserved only by you. For example, Federal Express believed Europe would be an easy market to conquer but discovered it was not. Limited volumes and intense competition in the overnight express parcel business made profitable competition untenable.

Conversely, Sea-Land Service, Inc., has avoided the kinds of problems associated with Federal Express' European experience. It has been a power in the container-sized shipping market because it astutely assesses a potential market's reaction to its quality, speed of service, pricing, and added capacity. Sea-Land will only tackle markets where its capacity utilization will be high without leading to a collapse of prices (and thereby margins) in the market. Where such conditions exist, it invests in developing its share of the market. But the potential of individual foreign markets clearly varies in many ways, such as openness to outsiders, currency stability, and degree of state ownership of industry. All of these factors, and others as well, influence the ability to enter a market profitably. Where it does not anticipate room to maneuver, Sea-Land will pass the market by, preferring to focus its skills and strengths on better prospects.[4] Similarly, until Coca-Cola mastered local distribution systems in Japan, its growth there was inhibited.

Multiple Approaches to Geographic Growth

There are several approaches to growing geographically. 3M and McDonald's invest in underdeveloped markets early on in hopes of preempting late-comers, to learn such markets well, and to develop the infrastructure and people to build more solid operations over time. For instance, both 3M and McDonald's were early investors in new operations in Russia, Poland, Czechoslovakia, Bulgaria and other former Soviet bloc countries.

Other companies such as Betz Laboratories do not invest in nations until they feel confident of a payoff from that nation's development. It was only in 1991 that Betz saw fit to invest in a factory in South Korea, after the country's industrial infrastructure had grown and become sufficiently sophisticated to be able to use Betz's services profitably. The less sophisticated an industrial infrastructure a country has, the less able it is to benefit from how Betz can improve its competitiveness and operations. For example, Betz's annual report states "A country must have a critical mass of industrial plants for the profitable growth of Betz business: And only in private, competitive markets does a return-on-investment market philosophy have any real meaning. The recent upheaval in the Soviet Union and Eastern Europe, with trends toward democracy and privatization, foreshadows additional opportunities but only in the long term." So Betz, unlike

McDonald's or 3M, will be a lot slower to move into Eastern Europe and Russia because its success depends on a relatively high level of industrial development.

McDonald's situation is different. It likes to move into markets early for another reason. It gets valuable experience about modifying its restaurants for cultural differences. For instance, it realized early on in Russia that its employees' "smiling" at customers was considered overly friendly. So it stopped doing this because it tended to unnerve its customers. In Japan it mixed a little fat and minced onions in its hamburgers and greatly boosted its sales success.

Still, a third approach is to treat markets as large zones rather than specific nations. The Disney Company is doing this as it builds its theme parks in Europe (EuroDisney in France) and Asia (Tokyo) in the hopes of drawing from more than just the host nation (Tokyo from Hong Kong and Singapore; EuroDisney from Spain, Germany, U.K., Italy, Holland, Belgium and even the Scandinavian nations).[5]

Yet a fourth approach is to grow business from core centers out, such as Blockbuster does by locating first in a country's larger cities and then expanding into medium-sized metropolitan centers. Ikea, the retail furniture giant, pursued this strategy, first close to home in Europe and then only later in North America and Asia. This $3.2 billion powerhouse (fiscal 1992) was founded in 1943 in Sweden and did not build a store outside Sweden until the 1960s. Yet, by 1974 it was in 5 other European nations; by 1984 it was in 17 countries all over the globe; and by 1992 it was in 24 countries (with 108 stores). However, 87 percent of its sales remain in Europe, still relatively close to its Scandinavian roots.[6]

As mentioned previously, Key Corporation takes a niche approach to geographic opportunity, specifically looking for underserved towns often with 10,000 or fewer people, often in geographically isolated states such as Utah, Alaska, Washington, and Wyoming.

International Marketing: Looking for Universal Formulas

Should the firm customize or standardize its strategy when planning to grow in foreign markets? The answer isn't clear-cut. While many global brands or retailers are succeeding with a fairly standardized approach, such as Caterpillar, Sony, Ikea, Benetton, and even Dell Computers, for every approach there is a company whose expansion is quite customized by market. Nestlé does not approach markets except on a custom basis, because many food tastes vary by nation. While universal needs exist for certain products such as beer, preferences obviously vary. The favorite beer sold in a nation varies markedly, even between countries as similar as Canada and the U.S. For other global products, such as photo film, videotape, or small batteries, customized marketing is less common and a standardized approach often works. It is interesting to note that Japanese car companies have sold "world" cars—a Toyota Corolla or Honda Accord is the same in Europe, in Japan or in North America—while American car companies have not been able to do this (though Ford tried and failed with its Escort). On the other hand, book publishing evidently is a long way from a globally standardized market. An October 1994 survey (by *The Economist*) of nonfiction bestsellers lists demonstrates the powerful pull of local tastes in the book business. In the survey of top ten selling nonfiction books in Germany, France, the U.K. and the U.S., not one single title appeared on more than one list. Only some fiction titles had success across national boundaries.

3M approaches many markets looking for buying preference similarities across nations. In this way, it has moved its marketing in Europe to emphasize regions where a Pan-European approach can apply. That is, it will market to target units larger than a nation but often smaller than the whole of Europe, based on broader groupings

The Growth Masters—New Locales

Company	*Product*	*Market*
Blockbuster Entertainment Corp.	Entertainment	Consumer
Key Corp.	Financial Services	Consumer/Business
Sea-Land Service	Shipping	Business
Ikea	Retail Furniture	Consumer
Betz Laboratories	Engineering	Business

of customers in southern, or northern, or central Europe. By approaching markets this way 3M avoids the excessive costs of total customization, while avoiding the pitfalls of standardizing its programs across too dissimilar a buying region.

Share Measurement: The Key to Growth

Whichever of the strategies outlined in this chapter you choose, it is important to invest in the ability to measure your growth by using the proper index. Growth via new users requires you to separate current from new users in order to be able to identify how many new users are coming into your total pool of customers each year. Cellular telephone companies do this in order to better understand developing user segments.

Growing by new uses (via application) requires a company to study its vertical markets and know how it is doing in each varied niche. Betz Laboratories makes a point of knowing its markets by application potential and then gauging its share in pulp and paper processing, steel mills, etc.

Lastly, growth via geographic expansion requires that a firm estimate market sizes for its chosen city, state, country or regional target. Only in this way can a company measure its performance accurately.

For example, this is the challenge facing the Disney Company. To be able to evaluate its regional strategy accurately, it needs to know whether it is drawing from just France (for EuroDisney) or from a wider trading area. In a service industry such as Disney's, this data reveals how well it is "pulling" customers in as well as how positive (or negative) word-of-mouth publicity (so key in entertainment industries), is playing out, by market, once its theme park visitors go back home. If certain visitor markets prove either more receptive or less receptive to its parks, it can look at how to improve its services to satisfy a greater percentage of its less impressed guests. Interestingly, EuroDisney customers, unlike Disney World U.S. visitors, usually get up early to go to the park and return home the same night. So while its geographic base of customers is large for "day" business, its overnight resort facilities' utilization is very poor because its European customers are culturally different from Americans (and can "same-day" drive home due to relatively shorter distances in Europe).

Summary

The common ground in growth in new markets through these three strategies is the ability to recognize opportunities. The companies discussed in this chapter creatively sought ways to leverage their past successes into future profits. A company does not have to reinvent the wheel; often it can sell that wheel to new users, for new uses, in new places.

Notes

1. "Nestlé: A Giant in a Hurry," *Business Week,* Mar. 22, 1993: 50, 51. Editorial.
2. Allan Magrath, "Deflationary Marketing," *Across the Board,* Jan./Feb. 1993: 33.

3. Gail De George, Jonathan Levine and Robert Neff, "Don't Call It Blockbuster for Nothing," *Business Week,* Oct. 19, 1992: 113, 114.
4. Milard Lele, "Exploiting Leverage," *Across the Board,* April 1993: 45–46.
5. See *Walt Disney Company 1991 Annual Report,* pp. 6–11, 19–21, on EuroDisney and Tokyo Disneyland respectively.
6. See Richard W. Stevenson, "Ikea's New Realities," *New York Times,* Sunday, April 25, 1993, 4F.

Chapter 3

Growing in Mature Markets

Increasing Total Market Share, Key Account Share, and Channel Share

> Consumers are making a structural change in their shopping habits—one that is likely to endure.
>
> *Fortune*
> "What Intelligent Consumers Want"
> Dec. 28, 1992, p. 57

Growth often must come from finding new product users, new product uses, or variations of these strategies, which all add up to creating, shaping, and responding to customer needs or serving them in new ways. But what about growing in mature markets, in which overall demand is static or possibly even declining? What variants to growth strategy exist here?

Aside from finding all new users or new products that reinvigorate the industry demand curve, there are three strategies to grow in markets for which demand has plateaued. These include taking market share from competitors on an across-the-board (total market) basis, entering strong customer partnerships through key account relationships, and growing, as well as gaining, market share by transforming or altering the marketing channels used to cover the market.

Total Markets, Total War

In a great many markets growth can only come by taking competitors' customers. Notable giants who compete for share this way include: Coke versus Pepsi; Gillette versus Schick versus Bic; AT&T versus Sprint or MCI; McDonald's versus Burger King or Wendy's; Kodak versus Fuji; Bridgestone/Firestone versus Goodyear and Michelin; Nike versus Reebok, and so forth.

Some of these very public battles for market share have even been given names. The "Cola Wars," the "Burger Wars," "Running Shoe Wars," and other such seemingly endless conflicts are fought on multiple fronts—in radio and television ads; in print; at the store-shelf and point-of-purchase levels; in stadiums and at special events and theme parks, in restaurants and vending machines—wherever there might be the chance to make just one more sale.

These share wars are often also waged over distribution loyalties. For example, tire brands compete head to head and side by side on dealer shelves for the dealer attention—for price featuring in ad flyers and for special attention by the in-store sales staff. In office equipment and supply products markets, manufacturers vie for share of display space—on the shelf, in the aisle, and at the point of purchase—against one another in powerful retail outlets such as Office Depot or Comp USA.

Changing Environments

Some market share battles are the result of governmental regulatory activity, where a new operating environment can create new competitors virtually overnight. For instance, MCI and Sprint have battled AT&T for share of the 800 number market in the U.S. ever since the Federal Communications Commission's (FCC) ruling that 800 numbers are transferable between long-distance carriers. The ruling, and the related court battle, created a new market with new competitors where there had been none.

The sudden appearance of a new competitor—the result of a decision to enter a new business—can similarly jump-start share wars. For instance, AT&T's decision to enter the credit card business has significantly reshaped competition in that industry. Similarly, the emergence of private label, store brands has had a major influence on the way some categories of packaged goods compete. Store brands have made significant inroads in supermarkets as branded products have crossed the price threshold in their markets. For example, in 1989, 16.4 percent of unit volume and 12.5 percent of supermarket dollar sales were private label, yet these numbers increased to 18.3 percent and 14 percent respectively in 1992, only three years later.

Retailers often do not view themselves as passive distributors of manufacturers' brands but as active marketers of proprietary store brands. Over 25 percent of the total annual sales of Carrefour, the giant French retailer, come from its own private label products. In just one category of intense competition—cereal sales—private label sales are growing 7 percent per year while sales of branded cereals such as Cheerios (General Mills) and Corn Flakes (Kellogg) are *declining* 5 to 6 percent per year as a result of too many price hikes in the 1980s and early 1990s.[1] Similar declining brand shares have forced both Procter & Gamble (Pampers diapers) and Philip Morris (Marlboro cigarettes) to cut prices of their leading brands in order to hold their market shares against generics and to give them the "value" prices customers desire. And pressure on health care costs has created a huge market for generic drugs—now approaching one-third of all prescriptions in the U.S. and Canada.

Tracking Customer Demands

Market share wars in no-growth industries require the absolute best market intelligence so that you sense and then know where customer preferences are and, perhaps more importantly, where they are headed. And success requires the ability to size-up competitors astutely—who they are and how they can be beaten.

Consider the retail women's apparel market. Consumer spending in this market has been flat since 1987, yet the number of specialty stores serving it has increased significantly. Those that read their customer needs correctly, such as The Gap and The Limited, prospered, rewarding shareholders with stock prices up by huge multiples since 1985. Others, such as Hartmarx Corp. and Gitano, either sold their specialty retailing divisions to more savvy competitors or simply closed huge numbers of stores. The customers wanted what The Gap and The

Limited had for sale and didn't want what Gitano and other stores offered.

But the only constant in retailing is change. Now in the nineties, as customers turn "down-market" for more discount brands at Kmart, Target, and Wal-Mart, The Gap and The Limited will be hard-pressed to duplicate their stellar performances of recent years. As one retail expert has said, "For ten years the country has been Gapped and Limited to the max, now customers are starting to buy their lookalikes at Wal-Mart and Lands' End. The same customer who buys an expensive sweater at St. John's now often buys her jeans at Kmart."[2]

On a more all-encompassing level, these kinds of competitors need to know where the total market is and where it's going. What the fashion retailers are facing is fundamental customer change—change driven by an aging population that is more middle-aged, more practical, and less driven by ego in clothing purchases. Share will go to those retailers able to offer distinctive quality at affordable prices. The retailers whose clothing is seen as either generic or unaffordable will lose share wars in the nineties. The classic success story at doing this is T.J. Maxx (514 stores) which sells brand-name women's, men's and kid's apparel at 20 to 50 percent below department store prices to time- and budget-conscious women in the 25 to 50 year old age group. T.J. Maxx' same-store sales and profits will grow by 12 percent in 1994 over the previous year, for the 17th consecutive year. It is interesting to note that in mid-1994 it was reported that The Gap was reconfiguring its merchandise mix in order to maintain its market position. Initial indications were positive.

Tracking Your Competitor

Aside from staying on top of customer shifts, companies that want to grow in static markets must keep a close eye on competitors and jump on any apparent weaknesses in their product line-up. Toys R Us and Home Depot dominate their retailing sectors because they operate on mark-ups that are one-half to two-thirds of those of traditional department stores or other competitors. They then dominate their competitors by offering lower prices to end consumers. More than 40 percent of all toys in America are now purchased at Toys R Us. Comp USA, a national computer superstore, offers brands such as Compaq or Apple at only a 13½ percent gross margin, far below competitors' mark-ups of 20 percent or higher. It is hardly any wonder that these electronic superstores are driving others out of business.

Chrysler, the proverbial "poor cousin" of the U.S. auto industry of the late 1970s and early 1980s, has done the same thing in a very different industry. When Chrysler's new LH cars were introduced, they stole significant market share from both Honda Accord and Ford Taurus because they offered more seating room and still preserved high styling. And they did so at competitive prices, giving consumers a value-driven combination of better price and quality that neither Honda nor Ford could match. Catching competitors napping has allowed the Chrysler Concord, Dodge Intrepid, and Eagle Vision models to far outgrow Ford and Honda's mid-size car growth rates. Chrysler's Neon model is an attempt to leapfrog their competitors' market shares in a similar fashion in the subcompact market segment.

Defining the Game

When total industry demand is static, it is imperative that you know your customers and know competitive openings. And it is equally important to have a sound sense of how share points are won. Depending on the characteristics of the market, this may mean gaining "share of mind," "share of shelf," "share of technology," or "share of selling effort."

Share of mind. In some markets (consumer goods in particular) gaining share of market means gaining "share of mind" among consumers. That elusive share of the "minds and hearts" of consumers is often a direct reflection of awareness, familiarity, and positive associations with the brand. Battles for this kind of awareness are usually fought in the media. Because a consumer can only remember a limited number of brands, the firm tries to ensure, through aggressive media weight (spending levels) and creative impact, that its brand is preeminent in the consumer's consciousness. Nike, Coca-Cola, Visa, and other long-time combatants in the "share wars" believe that share of market equals share of mind.

Most firms competing in such ways attempt to establish strong company names that can easily transfer across nations or product categories. Sony does this exceptionally well, as do Canon, Nestlé and Heinz. Their branding attempts to elevate the corporate name above that of individual products such as the Sony Walkman or the Canon copier. In this way consumers can be persuaded that the firm's reputation for quality in one field translates into another, creating a corporate reputation with which a private label generic brand can never compete.

Customers, of course, do not always buy into this notion, as Yamaha has found. Its fantastic reputation in musical instruments did not transfer into other markets such as skis, furniture, tennis rackets, or VCRs. But where a firm does do a good job of share-of-mind marketing, a corporate brand can dominate a brand arena and transfer that dominance to other product offerings. For instance, Sony is consistently mentioned as the number one brand in consumer electronics, a very broad catch-all category that includes audio, video, telecommunications, and other equipment. Nestlé has similarly managed to widely brand itself beyond the confines of chocolate into coffee and 400 other branded food categories.

Share of shelf. In other markets growth is much more a function of seizing the largest possible share of the resellers' floor or shelf space (i.e., retail distribution). The replacement tire market is a good example of this principle because tires tend to be either an emergency repair type purchase or a convenience purchase. In either case they must be on the shelf, ready for purchase. Thus, if Goodyear's tires are available in the most outlets or are in the largest concentration in any one outlet, it is Goodyear's tires that will go on the customer's car. When Goodyear made its tires available in Sears automotive centers, its overall share of the U.S. market increased, despite excellent availability of Goodyear tires in thousands of other convenient locations. Why? Because some Sears customers will always take their cars to Sears auto centers for their repairs, and the tire available on the shelf will command the sale, quite apart from any share-of-mind brand awareness Goodyear may have. Goodyear has also actively sought share of market by getting its products into Wal-Mart and Discount Tire.

Firms very skilled at understanding and playing the "shelf-presence" game include Wrigley's in the gum business, Mars in the candy business, and Kraft in the cheese and dairy products business. Each of these brands superbly manages its share of reseller space programs to make certain that it leads in total square footage and premium location for shopping traffic flow. WD-40, the maker of lubricants, dominates its market despite almost no consumer advertising because of its excellence in playing the share-of-shelf game.

Share of technology. In certain markets taking share is a result of having the widest technology acceptance. Losses or gains in share in these markets are almost entirely a result of changes in technology dominance. Xerox regained its share of market only after it regained its quality and technological prowess in copying. Boeing maintains world dominance in jetliner sales because it is the best in the world at mastering the technology of building world-class jet-passenger aircraft. And General Electric Medical Systems dominates the market share in medical scanners because it is the best in the world at medical imaging technology. Heavily invested in Beta technology, Sony lost market share to Panasonic and others when VHS became the format of choice.

This is not to say that these firms' products do not have to be priced competitively or marketed aggressively. But price and value are relative concepts. For instance, Boeing is selling its new 777 on value despite the $100 million price tag. The entire cabin, including seats, galleys and washrooms, can be completely reconfigurated in just 72 hours, a tremendous benefit to airlines. This kind of structural flexibility boosts an airplane's resale value because it can be converted quickly to a variety of uses (e.g., from cargo to passenger use or from short- to long-haul flights). Even in a consumer market such as newspapers, at was *USA Today's* use of satellite printing technology that enabled it to lead the industry in the production of a daily national newspaper incorporating color.

Share of quality selling effort. A firm may have identical products competing at identical pricing with identical competitors, but in one area it will have 85 percent market share and in another only 15 percent share of market. Why? Success in the share game often is a result of the proficiency of the firm's sales force. General Electric believes that its sales reps play this key role in many of its high-tech markets because they provide the differentiating advantage of a trusting relationship with the customer, whether it is for an aircraft engine or a high-tech plastic. General Electric's CEO of Medical Systems, John Trani, states it this way: "The human element is more important than ever. A buyer making a major investment wants to deal with a rock solid supplier. Companies will increasingly rely on people who can manage relationships, and great sales reps will pay a crucial role in the value decade of the nineties."[3] Research by BBDO, the advertising agency, on 4,000 customers in 28 countries for 14 different products (from beverages to personal computers) showed that as product advantages lessen between companies, customers decide on brand choices based on their comfort and trust with the sales rep who calls on them.

The Importance of Market Focus

Taking share as a way to grow often works best on a selective rather than on an industrywide basis. A firm may try to be the share leader in only one part of a market. For instance, Cooper Tire and Rubber deliberately does not compete in the original equipment tire market (tires put on new cars at the assembly plant), yet the company has produced shareholder returns in excess of 40 percent since 1985. Why? Because Cooper forgoes direct sales to auto makers at low margins and concentrates on excellent dealer sales into high-margin replacement tire markets.

Similarly, Apple Computer dominates the desktop publishing segment of computer technology. The highest growth company in the adhesives market is Loctite, which only tries to be the share leader in anaerobic adhesives, while one of its competitors, Henkel, a global company, prefers to do battle in multiple adhesive markets around the world. Thomas and Betts has a leading market share in electrical connecting products but does not play to nearly the same extent in electronic connectors, where Amp is the clear-cut share leader.

Paychex, based in Rochester, New York, dominates the payroll processing services business but only for small companies with fewer than 100 employees. Through tight market focus Paychex has grown since 1971 to $234 million in sales (1993 year-end) with 152,000 clients, with growth by market share expansion in its niche averaging compounded double digits for the last 20 years.

Defining and Measuring Your Markets

Companies using a market-share growth strategy must carefully enumerate in both units and dollar targets. Leadership in either one can produce profits—or losses. For instance, Marlboro and other premium brands have dominated the dollar share of the cigarette market. But as the low-margin discount cigarette segment grew from nothing 10 years ago to 33 percent of total units sold in 1992, it became apparent that regaining *unit share* had to be the priority of Philip Morris, owner of the Marlboro brand franchise. So the company cut prices in an attempt to regain unit share, where the key shift in share numbers has occurred.

Indirect forms of competition. Markets are defined by customer need and by the customer's use of the product rather than by the product's form. On one hand that statement seems transparently obvious, yet sometimes its accuracy plays out in unusual ways. For example, 3M competes in many markets in which its largest competitors are not makers of similar products but of alternate means of satisfying the customer's need. For instance, 3M's VHB (very high bonding) tape lines compete for automotive customers with rivets, screws, and other fastening devices such as clips that hold auto parts such as moldings to car bodies.

In these situations 3M defines its markets to include "indirect" competition, giving it a much more accurate, comprehensive, and larger target share to aim at. For example, only 10 percent of possible highway or intersection signing currently uses reflective sheetings, such as 3M's Scotchlite. The other 90 percent are still painted only and do not reflect light. Thus, while 3M is the share leader in *reflective* highway road sign materials, its major competitor remains the painted, nonreflective sign market, in which customers have not yet decided to reflectorize signs. This "indirect" part of the market actually represents the major part of 3M's market and its major source of competition.

Price points and value. Sometime it is useful to define market share targets based on price/value boundaries, that is, how much share the firm has of the low-, medium-, or high-end of the price-performance product spectrum. Until recently, Japanese auto makers had little or no presence in the luxury end of the automobile market but had solid share in the low-end and middle-priced market segments. They deliberately moved up market with the Lexus and other models, recognizing that their reputation for superb engineering and quality manufacturing could help them build a share here. IBM pursued this strategy in reverse when it launched its low-cost, very basic personal computer (Ambra) to compete for share head-on with the company's clone-manufacturing competitors.

Moving down market isn't always as easy or profitable as it might appear. Gucci moved down market in the 1980s and, by putting its name on 10,000 products (often without good quality), hurt its reputation in luxury products. Overall its sales and profits fell to the point that the firm had to be rescued by a 50 percent corporate share buy-out by InvestCorp International of Bahrain.

Using Maximum Creativity: Growing Share as a Small Player

The small-share marketer competing with giants faces a formidable challenge. It often lacks the resources necessary for huge advertising, sales force, or new product research and development outlays. This is where cleverness and creativity must help a company win out.

The Growth Masters—Total Market Share

Company	***Product***	***Market***
The Gap	Retail Clothing	Consumer
T.J. Maxx	Retail Clothing	Consumer
Toys R Us	Retail-Children's Toys	Consumer
Comp USA	Computers	Consumer/Business
Chrysler	Automobiles—Individual and Fleet	Consumer/Business
Nestlé	Food/Food Service	Consumer/Business
Goodyear	Tires	Consumer
WD-40	Lubricants	Consumer
Xerox	Office Systems	Business
Boeing	Aircraft	Business
General Electric	Medical Systems	Business
Cooper Tire and Rubber	Replacement Tires	Consumer
Paychex	Payroll Services	Business
Pick-Point Sports	Recreation-Golf	Consumer/Business
Black Entertainment Television	Entertainment	Consumer
Texaco	Oil Products	Consumer

Consider the case of Pick-Point Sports of Mirror Lake, New Hampshire, makers of golf balls that glow in the dark. Gaining market share in an industry dominated by the likes of Spalding and others is a tough task indeed, even with a gimmicky new product. So what did this small upstart do? It used inexpensive space ads in golf magazines to encourage golfers to get their clubs to sponsor "Nite Lite" tournaments—golfing after dark. Of course, the clubs can put on these events because Pick-Point's glow-in-the-dark golf balls make it possible to see at night. Since 1989, with a relatively meager ad budget (including rewards) of $150,000 per year it got 40,000 Nite-Lite golf tournaments off the ground around the world. From this activity 14,000 golf clubs

Case 5

Share-Taking in a Commodity Business: Texaco

Texaco, Inc., is prospering in the gasoline retailing business, despite flat total industry growth from 1989 to 1992 (approximately 115 billion gallons pumped annually throughout the period). In a business where a penny per gallon price difference can cause customers to switch brands, Texaco has grown its market share by 6 percent since 1990 at the expense of Shell and Exxon by using four key tactics:

1. It improved its fuels by launching cleaner burning gasolines (System 3), giving customers higher performance with fewer pollutants. Its diesel fuel has the lowest sulfur content of any on the market, making it very salable in environmentally sensitive states such as California.

2. It has spruced up 6,000 of its 14,000 gas stations (since 1990) by adding Texaco Star Marts, mini-marts that sell snack foods, beverages, and an expanding line of merchandise such as videocassettes. Stations with mini-marts attract more drivers and volume per station.

3. Texaco is beginning to add leased space for fast food franchises such as McDonald's and Dunkin' Donuts and for rapid lube facilities for "30 minutes-or-less" oil changes.

4. Texaco is reconfiguring its station network to cut gasoline transportation costs and thereby offer more competitive gasoline pump prices. It has organized its entire retail network for close proximity to its seven U.S. refineries. To accomplish this, Texaco is actively swapping outlets with other oil companies. For instance, it swapped 14 outlets in St. Louis for 15 Amoco stations in the Rocky Mountains region, closer to its refinery.

In effect, Texaco has altered its product, its services, its costs, and its total site attractiveness in an effort to grow its market share.

decided to stock Pick-Point's balls regularly and the company's sales grew to $10 million in three years (of which 17 percent is business outside the U.S.). This is the epitome of clever share taking at low cost in an industry dominated by giants.[4]

A small share-player needs to maximize its distinctive advantage to grow. In the television industry, one small-share player who demonstrates this is Black Entertainment Television, Inc., whose revenues top $68 million and profits $14 million in a business dominated by TBS, CBS, NBC, ABC, and Fox. Black Entertainment Television has uniquely positioned its programming for African-Americans' tastes and concerns. Music videos, news, and infomercials demonstrating products especially for the African-American community (such as skin care items for women) reach 36 million households per year. Similarly, MicroFridge of Sharon, Massachusetts, sells a patented combination microwave, freezer, refrigerator against the likes of G.E. and Whirlpool. It does well as a share player by concentrating on specialty customers such as university dormitories and seeking patents on its specialty lines.

Partnering with Key Accounts

An important variant of across-the-board or even segment share-taking growth strategy is growth via customer partnerships. In effect, the firm targets certain large customers in a deliberate effort to dominate their purchases to the exclusion of competitors. The most effective way to develop this strategy is to assist customer partners to grow *their* firm's business against the customer's competitors. The customer has all the characteristics of a key account, with mutual interests so entwined that the relationship functions as a partnership.

Levi-Strauss has such key partnerships with retailers such as J.C. Penney, as does G.D. Searle, the Monsanto Division that sells Nutra Sweet, to soft drink bottlers and other partners. Part of Nutra Sweet's marketing strategy is to convince end consumers of its customers' products to look for the Nutra Sweet symbol on the package. The goal of the strategy is to increase use of the Nutra Sweet ingredient by increasing use of the end product. In addition, the goal of such customer partnerships is to secure use of Nutra Sweet in as many of the customer's products as possible. So while Searle sells Nutra Sweet to General Foods as a partnership account for Jell-O Brand gelatin, Searle is also seeking the broadest possible use of the ingredient in all of General Foods' line of products from Tang drink mix to Kool-Aid and other items. Intel pursues an identical strategy to Nutra Sweet, for its computer chips with major electronics manufacturers. They attempt to get their high-speed chips in as many computer models made by a partner as possible while raising awareness with their "Intel inside" ads and logo.

Where the firm is a multiple-product manufacturer, it may seek to broaden its relationship with the key partner by selling more of its various lines to the customer. Baxter does this in the hospital market, selling all sorts of health care products from intravenous solutions to dressings to its key partner hospitals. 3M sells its aerospace customers such as Boeing not only its full line of tapes but also structural adhesives, safety products, abrasives, films, and a myriad of other items for use in aircraft or in its assembly process. So whether the customer (Boeing) or the vendor (Searle with Nutra Sweet) is single product dominated, the intent in any partnership is the same: to broaden either product applications or lines consumed by the customer partner. Cummins Engine Company of Columbus, Indiana ($3.5 billion in sales) has such a strong customer partnership with Ford Motor Company as a supplier of diesel engines for Ford trucks that Ford decided to buy 27 percent of Cummins' stock for $250 million.

Case 6

Sometimes It Isn't the Product: American Distribution Systems' Service-Based Partnering

While building partnership bridges often emphasizes products and product manufacturing capabilities, as in the Cummins-Ford partnership, this isn't always the case. A firm can grow a partnership by offering special service capabilities. American Distribution Systems, a specialized carrier delivery firm, partnered with CIBA-Geigy's pharmaceutical division to deliver all CIBA drug samples through its contracted independent truckers network. American Distribution Systems guarantees that CIBA's nationwide sales force receives samples within a specified two-hour window anywhere in the continental U.S. (or CIBA-Geigy doesn't pay), while guaranteeing that the sales rep has signed for the drugs (a legal requirement to keep drugs from finding their way into the illicit drug trade).

American Distribution Systems not only has gained all of CIBA's business by keeping to this promise on delivery, it also sustains the partnership by:

- Providing CIBA with the ability to trace any samples anywhere in the distribution pipeline;
- Giving CIBA on-line computer access to American Distribution Systems' computer network;
- Providing toll-free, fax-free ordering on American Distribution Systems that allows for instant routing changes for rep pick-up destinations or changing volume or mix needs.

So key are these linkages from American Distribution Systems to CIBA that American Distribution Systems got one hundred percent of CIBA's business and charged at premium prices over other lower cost but less service flexible delivery services.

The Problems with Partners

The American Distribution Systems/CIBA-Geigy partnership provides a good working model of how well partnerships between companies can work. But partnerships between companies of unequal size are problem-prone since dependence is clearly not mutual. IBM and General Motors have been renowned for dominating partnerships with their suppliers, often to the partner's detriment. These huge customers have played hardball with suppliers so often that the level of trust disintegrates. And lack of trust often destroys partnerships.

As Jerrold Kaplan, CEO of Go Corp., told the *New York Times* about his Silicon Valley company's partnership with IBM: "When the elephant dances with the cat, it has to be careful where it steps and the cat has to be nimble."[5] The Marketing Science Institute study of partnerships concluded that while alliances of this sort offer "fresh opportunities to reach new markets," partnerships between small firms and big ones are very risky, calling the "wisdom of such partnerships" into question.[6]

Nevertheless, in some markets, share growth without partnering with key accounts is almost impossible. For example, in U.S. toy markets, failure to sell your toy to Toys R Us can mean no growth or curtailed market potential or total failure due to the retailer's dominance of retail toy sales. Cap Toys Inc., of Bedford Heights, Ohio, was one of the top 100 fastest growing firms on *Inc.* magazine's 1992 list, despite competing against Mattel, Hasbro, and other toy giants. If Toys R Us doesn't like a toy, Cap Toys won't manufacture it. Cap Toys' owner and president meets with Toys R Us prior to all new product launches and discusses the toy's concept, packaging, and pricing with his retail partner and modifies it as his partner suggests. Despite the vagaries of toy manufacturing success, Cap has grown its sales to Toys R Us into the multimillions. Cap Toys' attitude is that Toys R Us knows what sells, and if they look at three thousand toy concepts before they find ten or twelve they like, why shouldn't they run these ten or twelve past their largest most successful customer?

Exhibit 3–1 diagrams conceptually how a partnership typically differs from key account selling. The most complex partnerships involve a supplier partnering with its distributors *and* in turn with the ultimate end-use customers. For instance, Emerson Electric would partner with a distributor such as W.W. Grainger, which then in turn partners with a key account for electric motors, such as Hoover Vacuum or General Electric's appliance division. These partnerships are tricky since the opportunities for missed communications or foul-ups exist on three dimensions, both ways (or six information flows).

Exhibit 3–2 diagrams the flows between and among the firms and shows how communication issues could arise on matters such as pricing, product warranties, logistics, services, or promised product performance. To make complex three-way partnerships work best, it is ideal to sort out the roles, expectations, and functions each partner expects of the others and to adjust these over time to reflect the value-added concerns of the ultimate customer (in this case, General Electric).

Some partnerships do not work, of course, because "it takes two to tango," and sometimes one firm refuses partnerships as a matter of policy. This is the case with the Food Lion Supermarket chain, which won't partner even with the likes of Quaker Oats or Pillsbury, believing that using buyers to cut deals with multiple vendors is what keeps them competitive (rather than using fewer key vendor partnerships).

A considerable degree of openness and cooperation is required to grow share by partnership. The focus must be on the longer term (versus the last transaction). Exchanges of information, broader services, and product lines must be fine-tuned as the partners learn to trust one another. Typical confrontational and manipulative buyer-seller

Exhibit 3–1
Partnerships versus Key Account Selling: Nature, Depth, and Scope of Contacts

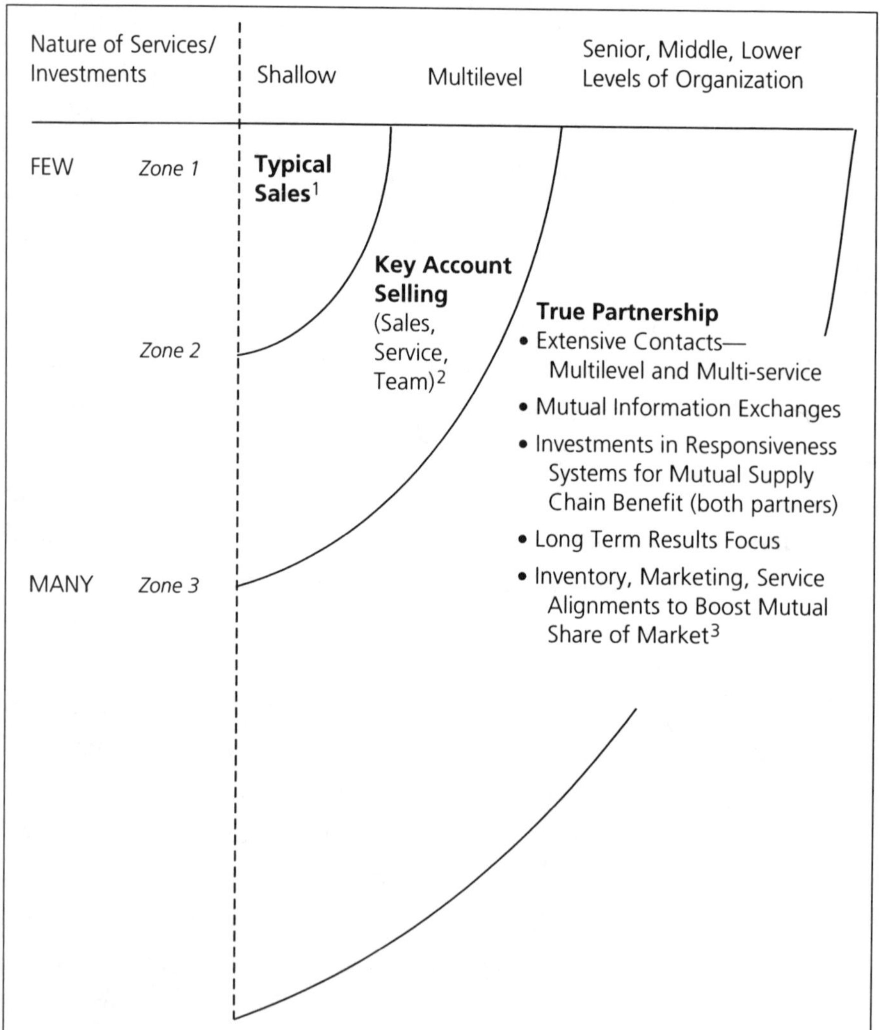

[1] Zone 1: Shallow contacts, few services
[2] Zone 2: Multiple contacts, some services
[3] Zone 3: Partnering zone, many contacts and services

Exhibit 3–2
A Three-Way Partnership and Its Six-Way Flows

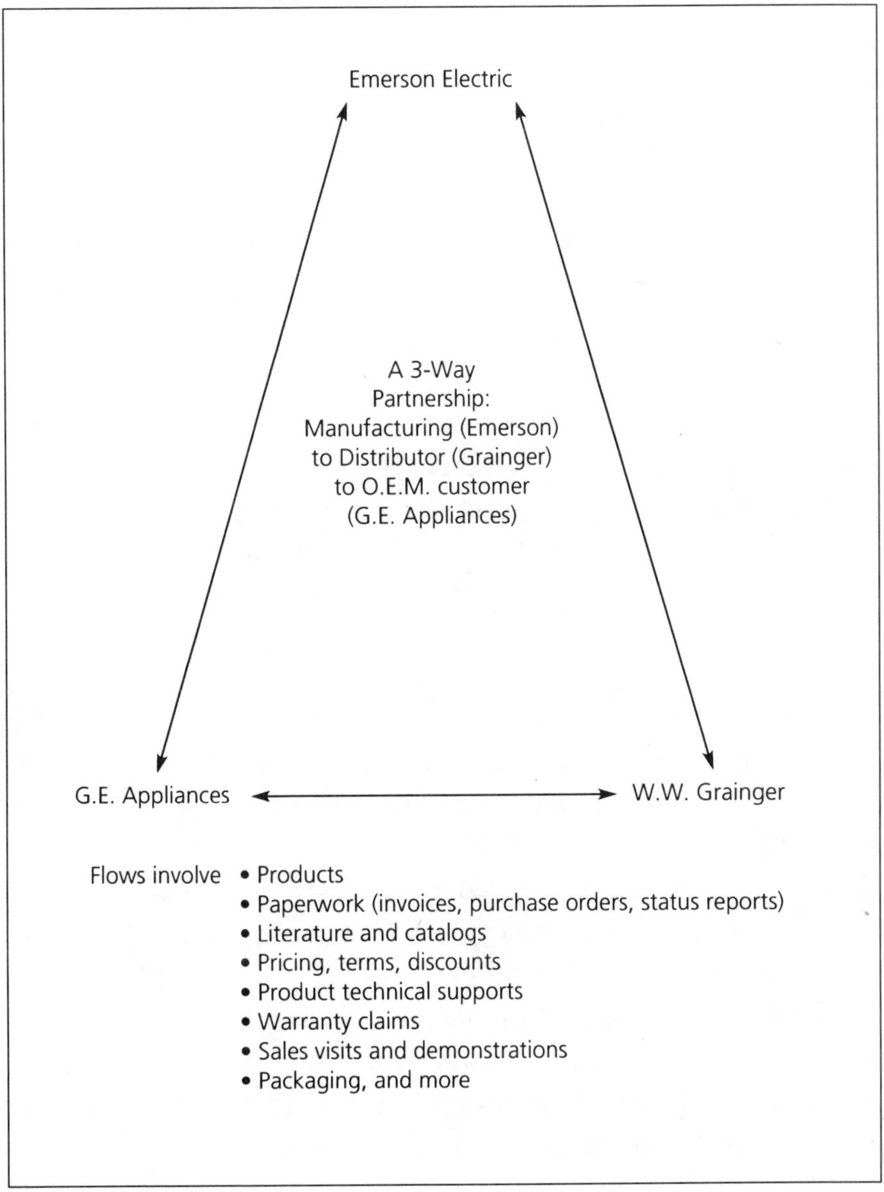

The Growth Masters—Key Account Partners

Company	*Product*	*Market*
Levi-Strauss	Clothing	Consumer
Monsanto/G.D. Searle	Food	Consumer/Business
Baxter International	Medical	Business
American Distribution Systems	Transportation/Delivery	Business
Cap Toys	Toys-Children	Consumer
Procter & Gamble	Packaged Goods	Consumer
Kmart	Mass Market Retail	Consumer

attitudes must be set aside. Tyson Foods' partnerships with fast food chains led it to create Chicken McNuggets for McDonalds and "Rotisserie Gold," KFC's new hit product.

In another instance, Procter & Gamble and Kmart decided to partner to cut total distribution costs and to allow for responsive store-specific marketing and product mix strategies. To make it work, they had to get CEO-level support from both sides. They shared information on costs, margins, market share, and net profits, all previously considered totally confidential in their former nonpartnership mode. And they each had to boost information system spending *prior* to realiz-ing system cost savings. In other words, they invested in extra short-term costs requiring lots of mutual trust and patience before benefits were forthcoming. The partnership led to cross-functional teams from both firms interacting daily on accounting, MIS, buying, advertising, order entry, and warehousing. So far the relationship has yielded increased profits and cash flow for both, lower total system inventories, a 99 percent-plus in-stock service record, higher customer satisfaction among consumers, and cost reductions in warehousing, order and inventory handling, obsolescence, and interest/space costs.

Cross-Border Customer Partnerships

Boosting growth with strategic account partnerships gets more complex when the supplier-customer relationship crosses national political boundaries. When pan-regional or global partnerships are pursued, they often involve the subsidiaries of both companies. For instance, 3M supplies diaper tape closures on a global basis to Procter & Gamble for use in its Luvs and Pampers products, which are made in several countries.

Three issues require high levels of coordination to make such a partnership successful. First, pricing must be standardized across the various regions and prices denominated in the customer currency of choice. Once a benchmark currency is selected, the value of the currency relative to the various countries in the network is adjusted up or down as customer plants in different countries are supplied by the local subsidiary of the supplier.

Second, supply chain service standards negotiated globally or regionally must be met by the local supplier partners relative to delivery specifications, labeling, packaging, invoicing and product match-ups for the local customer's factory needs. Often, the customer wants the supplier to meet excellent benchmarked service standards, regardless of the local supplier's set-up, as a quid pro quo for the global business.

Third, sales and technical support to the various customer plants around the world must be coordinated so that the customer gets the help and support it needs, including "trouble-shooting" if necessary. In effect, global customers exchange money for a set of skills, services, and products whose excellence must be demonstrated to all the customer's manufacturing locations around the world.

Ford Motor Company is in the process of moving to global purchasing in order to drive down its costs and increase the number of cross-border buying partnerships the company will conclude. Having fewer vendors allows Ford to leverage the scale of its buying power and gives it the ability to spend less management time on vendor negotiations and more on training and working with fewer, more dedicated quality vendors.

Growth Through Channel Share

Channel control clearly is important to success in growth by share acquisition. Selecting the best channel to your customer is also key. Sometimes it means creating whole new ways to reach your customer; sometimes it means doing things new only to you; and sometimes it means working more effectively in channels you've already developed.

A company can increase market share by finding new pathways to customers previously not available to it. In effect, the company jumps to new distribution channels and rides them to successful share-taking. Grey Poupon mustard unlocked fresh growth opportunities through restaurant food service channels, a previously untapped pathway to market. Another example is Taco Bell, which was the first fast food franchise to put outlets in previously untapped channels such as airports, sports stadiums, and even convenience stores. By doing so, it increased market share by 37 percent. The company is even experimenting with street carts and vending machines.

In a very different industry, drug companies are beginning to sell through mail order channels, which are growing in volume by 33 percent per year. Such well-known retail chains as Walgreen's and Thrift Drugs (owned by J.C. Penney) have started up mail order delivery operations. Merck was so concerned with access to this new mail order channel for drugs that it bought Medco, the largest mail-order drug firm in the U.S., for $6 billion.

Phillips Van Heusen Corp., a clothing and footwear manufacturer, owes much of its recent growth to its shift in channels. It is a big name in factory outlet malls across the U.S. and sells $550 million alone in such outlets, up from zero 10 years ago. More than 175 U.S. communities now have such malls, up 17 to 18 percent from 1991–92 alone. In 1988, there were only 3,786 apparel outlets in such malls, but by 1992 8,640 such outlets were in operation. Fifty percent of Van Heusen's sales come from such malls, while two-thirds of its profits come from this emerging channel (via 630 stores under the Van Heusen, Bass, Cape Isle Knitter, Geoffrey Beene and Windsor Shirt names). Factory outlets, once home to factory seconds or manufacturers' overruns, are now mainstream retail attractions selling upscale brands at 20 percent below standard retail prices. Many such outlets attract carloads of families and friends to brand names such as Liz Claiborne, Nike, Polo, Mikasa, J. Crew, Dansk, and Donna Karan.

New Channels/New Ways

While some firms can jump-start their growth by aligning themselves with new channels, sometimes the growth solution is simpler; just expand your channels beyond self-imposed, narrow confines.

For many years Compaq computer had a channel strategy of selling only through independent computer dealers, ignoring other well-established channels for computers, such as computer superstores and mail-order. Today that has all changed. Compaq tripled its channels by signing up Comp USA, Circuit City, and Office Depot and now also sells by direct response (i.e., catalog mailings and telemarketing). Compaq's moves have expanded their narrow channel coverage from 3,300 outlets to 8,800 outlets worldwide, helping to rebuild its share and reap the coverage advantages for its new models of Prolinea computer. Apple Computer has also expanded its channels for more share, now selling corporate accounts direct, and has added mail order and mass merchants to its traditional 1,500 resellers.

While both these computer firms' core dealers resisted these moves, the companies have been forced by customer choice to sell their computers where customers wanted to buy them—by direct response and in other retail outlets.

Hallmark Cards is faced by a similar dilemma: Depending too heavily on specialty card shops for their sales rather than convenience channels, such as drugstores, grocery or discount chains. Card buyers increasingly do not make a separate trip to a card specialist but, rather, pick up a card when also buying food or drug items, and Hallmark's competitors are exploiting Hallmark's poor presence in convenience outlets. For instance, American Greetings' sales growth and profit improvement are surpassing Hallmark's due to these convenience channels.

Electronic Channels

What better time to think about saving money than when you're at the bank? That's part of the rationale driving the ATM program developed by EFT Promotions of Dunwoody, Georgia. The program offers an interesting twist on the practice of giving coupons for competing brands at retail checkout.

The EFT program provides four-color coupons attached to depositors' ATM receipts. McDonald's, Burger King, and Jiffy Lube were among the first to test the program. They were joined shortly by Firestone, KFC, Precision Tune, and others. Each coupon rotates for three- to five-month periods with *non*competing brands. It's a simple, but effective, use of electronic channels.

The Growth Masters—Channel Share

Company	***Product***	***Market***
Philips Van Heusen Corp.	Clothing	Consumer
Merck/Medco	Pharmaceuticals	Consumer
Compaq	Computers	Consumer/Business
American Greetings	Greeting Cards	Consumer

Channel Control as a Competitive Edge

Tight channel control can shut out or deter competitors. For instance, A&W Brands grew to number five in the $47 billion U.S. beverage market by hitching-a-ride on the bottling and distribution networks of Coca-Cola and Pepsi,[7] which did not offer competitors to A&W's Root Beer, Cream Soda, and Country Time Lemonade. However, as A&W begins introducing new products that threaten to compete with Coke and Pepsi (such as Tetley iced tea, which competes with Coke's Nestea, and Everlast Sports drink, which competes with Pepsi's All Sport), the Coke and Pepsi bottlers are not free to bottle these directly competing brands (due to control by Coke and Pepsi in their bottler agreements). So Coke and Pepsi's bottler affiliations will likely greatly hamper A&W's share-taking plans with new competing beverages. As a result the company will need to use far less powerful bottler connections (such as second-tier bottlers), to cover its markets with its brands.

Better Training

Sometimes growth through channels can come from teaching established channels how to market better. DuPont has done a superb job of teaching its carpet dealers to sell its Stainmaster Carpet, making it a worldwide success. Movie studios are only just beginning to work with Blockbuster and other retail video chains to teach them how to better merchandise and sell-through new movie releases on video (most of Blockbuster's sales revenue is from movie rentals).

Lighting manufacturers such as General Electric, Philips Lighting, and GTE/Sylvania are teaching department and specialty stores how to sell lighting products as home decor enhancers that improve the look of rugs, furniture, artwork, and draperies. These firms feel retailers lack skills to position lighting products for decorative purposes, a key part of a home improvement appeal. As customers build fewer homes and spend more time and money redecorating the ones they have, these lighting manufacturers feel their retailers should capitalize on this basic trend by selling the benefits of light for creating shadows, space, and accents on walls, rugs, and furnishings, rather than selling the lights themselves.

Summary

As industries mature, firms within such markets must find new ways to grow or risk stagnant sales and profits—or even extinction. Three of the most effective ways are to take share from direct rivals by means of more effective presence in and communication with the total market, to marry-up with strategically important accounts via partnerships, or to look for different channels of distribution. Those that can master such strategies are renewing their growth while others who do not are losing share—of markets and of profits—to more nimble, open-minded rivals.

Notes

1. Thane Peterson, "Snap, Crackle, Flop?" *Business Week,* May 10, 1993: 34. Data from Information Resources Inc., 52 weeks from March 1991 to March 1992.
2. Gretchen Morgenson, "Here Come the Cross Shoppers," *Forbes,* December 7, 1992: 160. Quotes Allan Millstein, a New York City Fashion Consultant.

3. Stratford Sherman, "How to Prosper in the Value Decade," *Fortune,* Nov. 30, 1992: 103.
4. Susan Greco, "Product Launches," *Inc.,* Nov. 1992: 29.
5. Martin Everett, "Why Partners Sometimes Part," *Sales and Marketing Management Magazine,* April 1993: 73.
6. *Ibid.,* 70,73. MSI report is quoted.
7. Elizabeth Lesley, "A&W's Summer Plans: Hitting the War Path," *Business Week,* April 12, 1993: 53, 54.

Chapter 4

Growing Through Brand Extensions

Licenses, Flankers, and Line Assortments

Deciding on the optimum market variety is part of an interactive process that never really ends . . . in order to optimize the level of variety the decisive lever is value in the customer's eyes.

Sloan Management Review,
Review of *The Management of Complexity,* by Peter Child, R. Diederichs, T.H. Sanders, S. Wisniowski
Fall, 1991, p. 73

Every executive works to create a "cash cow"—a product that takes and holds a significant share of its market and performs profitably year after year. Unfortunately, every company faces two major hurdles in creating this kind of money machine. First, the cost of entry into new markets is higher than ever and the level of competition is more intense than ever. Second, customers are more demanding and less loyal than ever. The three strategies discussed in this chapter show how it is possible to jump these hurdles to higher market share and greater profits. First, licensing can help firms enter new markets at low cost or, conversely, provide additional products for markets they already serve profitably. And the second and third strategies, creating flankers and line assortments, enable a company to create maximum product diversity at minimum expense.

Licensing

In the U.S., 1992 sales of licensed products topped $62 billion, and some parts of the market such as sports licensing are growing at 12 percent per year. Sales of products licensed by the National Football League (NFL), the National Basketball Association (NBA), the National Hockey League (NHL), and Major League Baseball grew from just over a billion dollars in 1987 to more than $6.6 billion in 1992. In 1993, the NBA alone will sell $250 million in licensed merchandise into overseas markets from Australia to Turkey and Taiwan.

The licensing of brand identities to expand sales is a proven winning strategy for a great many product categories, from sports logos to luxury goods. Consider Starter Corporation, founded in 1974 as a maker of team uniforms for high schools. Licensing professional sports team logos, Starter manufactures shirts, caps, and jackets bearing NFL, NBA, and Major League Baseball trademarks. Its sales grew from $120 million in 1990 to more than $360 million in 1993. Its premium parkas and jackets, made from satin and leather, rather than cheaper nylon, sell for as much as $200. It pays 8 to 10 percent of sales to the license holders for the rights to use the logos on its clothing and hats. It is a win-win strategy: Starter Corp. grows as Major League licensing sales and revenues also expand.

Product Diversification

The success of licensing of logos has gained acceptance for licensing in more and more product categories. Sports league merchandise licenses used to be confined to a few products, such as trading cards, souvenir programs and traditional caps, jerseys, and jackets. But today, sports licenses are sold for children's clothing, women's apparel, commemorative sports memorabilia (figurines of famous players), and all sorts of home videotapes (of championship games, goofy plays, etc.).

Hollywood has seized on this licensing tactic with a frenzy. Consider the case of *Batman,* the 1989 Warner Brothers film. While it earned over $241 million at the box office, licensing revenue was twice that much—$500 million—by licensing the Batman logo for T-shirts, coffee mugs, sound track albums, cereal, and premiums of nearly every description offered by McDonald's, Sears, and other retailers. Even the Six Flags Theme Parks opened a new attraction dubbed "Batman the Ride."[1]

Licensing has spread well beyond clothes, toys, collectibles, greeting cards and sports items to include such products as small personal care appliances. Conair, a leader in manufacturing hair dryers and curling irons, licensed the "Beverly Hills 90210" name to use on its products, and Helen of Troy, a Conair competitor, licensed Vidal Sassoon's trademark, getting a leading market share in personal care appliances from this tactic. In addition, it has licensed the Revlon name to grow its sales even more.

Case 7

Licensing as a Way to Boost Sales and Profits: Lifetime Hoan Corporation

Lifetime Hoan Corporation is a $65 million (sales), $7 million profit-generating producer of kitchen knives, potato peelers, and muffin tins. It sells to Macy's, Wal-Mart, Caldor, Lechter's, and other retail chains and mass merchandisers. In 1990, when its sales were only in the $50 million range and profits were less than two-thirds of current levels, it decided to boost its "commodity producer" brand image by licensing the Farberware brand from Hanson PLC in England. Farberware knife and cutlery sets sell for three times more than Hoan's brands, yet it sells to the same retailers as Hoan does.

By licensing the Farberware line, Hoan broadened its hold on its customers with the addition of the premium line of cutlery to its budget-minded brand and boosted its sales by 25 percent in three years. In addition, Farberware's premium pricing and higher margins produced profits on those sales of nearly 35 percent. Furthermore, sales to some of Hoan's more specialized accounts such as Bed Bath and Beyond doubled since these kinds of retailers are more upscale than Wal-Mart. The lesson to be learned: Licensing as a strategy can lift both the top and bottom lines for the license holder while also strengthening its hold on its current customers.

Why Licensing Works

Licensing is considered a way of tapping into new markets without cannibalizing existing products. Helen of Troy was able to gain additional shelf space from retailers for the "new" licensed "Vidal Sassoon" name and still maintain the shelf space it had for its own nonlicensed products.

Licensing on an international basis offers the ability to transfer brands across borders into new markets with great speed. Playboy Enterprises has been able to move aggressively into Eastern Europe through licensing deals. It has entered Poland, Hungary, and Czechoslovakia by means of licensed sales with Eastern European publishers, such as Warsaw-based VIPress, which has a 50/50 joint venture with Playboy. The venture's Polish magazine, launched in December 1992, sold 100,000 copies in two days.

Licensing can be a very profitable long-term strategy. Sanyo Fashion House of Japan holds a 20-year license to produce and sell Burberry of London's clothing in Japan and today generates more than $1 billion in sales of this line. Burberry's is so pleased by the growth and profits from this licensing arrangement that it is expanding its activities to U.S. and Canadian markets. Sanyo will sell and manufacture jackets, shirts, pants, shorts, and woven blouses with Burberry's name from its Oneonta, New York, factory for sale to department and specialty stores across North America.[2]

Quality Risks

The lure of licensing is seductive, but it poses great dangers, especially to luxury goods manufacturers. Since the 1970s, perfumes, cosmetics, watches, jewelry, leather goods, crystalware, chinaware, automotive accessories all have been sold using licensed brand names. By diluting exclusivity, many brands, such as Yves St. Laurent, Christian Dior, and Pierre Cardin, have lost their luster—and sales.

The use of licensing as a growth tactic must strike a balance between "milking" brand images and ruining them. In luxury goods, too wide an availability of the brand or too downscale a product upon which the logo appears can only spell a loss in brand prestige and hurt the snob appeal that contributes to the success of such products. In the mid-1980s, Gucci had put its brand (via licensing) on 14,000 different products from key chains to sun glasses and coffee mugs. By stretching its brand names beyond the breaking point, the company irreversibly damaged its name, and its sales and profits have never recovered.

The issue often is control. While licensing often produces growth, the license holder can lose control of the quality of the products that flow from the licensee. Licensing deals granted by Yves St. Laurent and Christian Dior to make ties and socks proved disastrous when some of the manufacturers cut corners on quality in both the sewing construction and choices of materials and fabrics. Shoddy licensed products have also hurt Ralph Lauren's Polo brand and IZOD's Lacoste brand when they were rolled out internationally.

Licensing can also create counterfeiters who thrive on making knock-offs that are very tough to tell superficially from the real thing. Cartier, the luxury watch manufacturer, has one person in Paris whose sole responsibility is to keep tabs on its watches. The Swiss watch industry calculates annual losses of more than one billion Swiss Francs due to sales of counterfeit watches.[3]

Despite the inherent risks in licensing, it can provide sources of revenue and market presence that are absolutely vital to success and, sometimes, existence. For example, in an area very different from those discussed previously, U.S. universities have turned to licensing their logos and found whole new revenue sources to help them balance their budgets during difficult economic times. The University of Michigan generates in excess of $5 million in licensing fees from their popular logo on hats, clothes, sports bags, and knapsacks. Similarly, until the Olympics got into the full swing of licensing, it was leaving over $2 billion in revenue untapped.

So licensing does represent a way to grow sales, and every firm should consider a brand, product or technology license to boost its revenue in new market segments, in new international markets, or in new product categories.

Harley-Davidson is a good case in point. A generation ago it was in serious financial difficulty. Today, the company sells a complete line of biker accessories, clothing, and lifestyle gear manufactured by others under license—in addition to the most distinct line of motorcycles in the world. These accessories allow its riders to customize their bikes and go to Harley Owner Group rallies, all in similar Harley gear. In Tokyo, Harley has two stores that sell nothing but these clothes and accessories.[4] This strategy has helped the company keep its identity strong in a market noted for generics and to keep its overall bike sales up.

Making the Most of Your Message

Line extensions and licensing of brand names have been staples of packaged goods makers for many years. But now licensing is being used in the unlikely category of magazine publishing. And the leader isn't some innovative, high-flying newcomer to the industry. It's Hearst Magazines, which has been publishing for more than a century.

Hearst licenses the names of its publications, such as *House Beautiful, Good Housekeeping, Sports Afield,* and *Popular Mechanics.* The strategy is to go beyond merely creating a brand extension to creating involvement in the lifestyle of the brand and the brand user. The key to success, explains David Graff, vice president and director of brand development for Hearst, the company's strategy involves much more than just putting a name on a product: ". . . It's important to incorporate brand image as much as possible. If you stay true to your market, you'll have plenty of flexibility."

And lots of success. Hearst's four basic tactics—trademark licensing, archival licensing, home video, and new media—produce $500 million in annual revenue. The company's largest retail licensee is Wal-Mart. Products run the gambit from *House Beautiful* paints to

The Growth Masters—Licensing

Company	***Product***	***Market***
Starter Corp.	Clothing	Consumer
Conair	Personal Care Appliances	Consumer
Helen of Troy	Personal Care	Consumer
Playboy	Publishing	Consumer
Sanyo Fashion House	Clothing	Consumer
Lifetime Hoan	Kitchenware	Consumer
Harley-Davidson	Motorcycles	Consumer
Motorola	Wireless Communications	Consumer/Business

Popular Mechanics tools, to *Redbook* exercise videos to *Esquire* watches and *Good Housekeeping* greeting cards and calendars—and more.

Technology Licensing

While licensing is best known in the branded consumer products game, it is also used by industrial and high-tech manufacturers as a way to grow quickly. Motorola, for example, has licensing alliances with AT&T, Cray Research, Apple Computer, and Mitsubishi. By entering into cross-licensed technology deals, Motorola has transformed itself from a consumer electronics company into the recognized world leader in wireless communications.

The use of licensing is not confined to trademarks but can include product designs, process trade secrets, and a variety of "know-hows" tied to products and their manufacture. As knowledge and technology transfer accelerates on a global scale, the amount of licensing will no doubt increase. For example, licensing of drug formulations between pharmaceutical companies has been commonplace for many years, but today, as certain drugs lose patents, the patent holders are licensing formulations to consumer products companies more skilled in over-the-counter medication markets, in which these drug companies have little marketing or sales experience. The drug company works with a consumer products firm to develop an over-the-counter nonprescription variant of the drug, which generates additional sales and profits from the formulation. This strategy becomes critical because competitive generic drug makers can enter the market after the patent expires and gain share through low-priced clones. Licensing the formulation for over-the-counter use becomes an offsetting growth strategy that generates new revenue and at the same time combats the loss of prescription business to the generic competitors.

Growth Through Flanker Brands

Holding rights and extending the brand franchise across complementary products with the company is yet another platform for growth. Flanker brands extend a brand name to another category of product or service for which such an image transfer makes sense.

Michelin, whose main business is tire manufacturing, is the leader in producing and selling European maps and guidebooks for travelers, an offshoot that exploits the French Michelin brand presence throughout Europe.

General Motors developed a very imaginative flanker for the financial services area. The GM brand spin-off is a no-annual-fee "affinity" credit card offered in conjunction with VISA. The affinity card has a service and sales dimension: it helps potential customers accumulate future sales credits for car purchases from General Motors. For every credit card purchase using the card, General Motors accumulates 5 percent of the value of the sale in an account that a car buyer can use to buy a General Motors automobile. This sort of flanker brand adjunct to its car business produced one million card sign-ups in 38 days in 1993. By the early spring of 1993, 7,500 General Motors cars and trucks had been sold or leased with the rebate-linked General Motors affinity card.

There are many examples of flanker brands from the packaged goods industry. Procter & Gamble launched "Simply JIF," a low-salt, low-sugar version of its Jif peanut butter aimed at diet-conscious buyers; and Gillette introduced a new line of deodorants, shaving creams, and aftershaves under the successful Sensor razor brand umbrella. There is an additional dimension to Gillette's strategy: It is trying to exploit its huge global success with the Sensor brand to do a better job in toiletries, where it has not been very successful. Though its toiletries currently generate 20 percent of all Gillette's sales, they represent only half this percentage (12½%) of total corporate profits. By linking the Sensor name to allied products, the company not only hopes to get more market share but also to boost pricing for these items consistent with Sensor's "quality" brand image.

With the same idea in mind 3M capitalized on the success of its ubiquitous Post-It notes brand name to launch "Post-It" tape flags and "Fax Notes," two flanker products that use post-it "technology" in new ways. Tape flags provide high-visibility page markers for documents, while fax notes label and signature fax messages, eliminating the need for a separate cover page.

Launching flanker brands usually is a less expensive, and therefore, a more attractive, method of going after a new market niche than launching an all-new unknown brand. General Mills, for example, makes both Yoplait yogurt and Trix children's cereals. It decided it wanted to extend its success in yogurts by targeting children six to eleven years old. It discovered through market research that kids strongly identified with its Trix Rabbit, so General Mills launched a new line of Yoplait yogurts for children using the Trix brand identity. The strategy is clear: Combine its brand equities to raise the sales of yogurt to kids. Using a proven brand name transfer also saved General Mills time to market. Its Trix Yoplait was brought to market in just six months from invention to appearance in stores. The brand raised Yoplait's share by 3 points—more than $70 million in sales.

Stretching Brand Names to the Limit

As product variety increases with line extensions, the law of diminishing returns applies. At a certain level of variety, consumers become confused or distribution channels become clogged.

Fruit of the Loom is a fine example of brand extension-based growth, because it did not extend its brand beyond its logical limitations (for instance into higher fashion underwear, where in fact it uses a different brand name, "Munsingwear"). Similarly, Philip Morris, owners of Kraft General Foods, Miller Brewing and various tobacco brands has demonstrated the principle of controlling brand extension growth. It extended the Miller Brand franchise (Miller High Life) first into Lite beers (Miller Lite) with great success. It then extended it further into the draft bottled beer category with Miller Genuine Draft and Genuine Draft Lite (which in 1992 was America's seventh most popular beer).

Recognizing the dangers of overextending the franchise, when it came to launching a non-alcohol beer the company did so with the brand name Sharp's. This tactic proved very astute: Sharp's is growing at a rate of 30 percent per year and is the number one brand in the non-alcohol category. Philip Morris recognized that even though it could stretch its Miller franchise from premium beer (High Life) to low cal and then draft categories, when it went into non-alcohol beer it was

The Growth Masters—Flankers

Company	***Product***	***Market***
Michelin	Maps	Consumer
General Motors	Financial Services (GMAC)	Consumer
Procter & Gamble	Food	Consumer
Gillette	Personal Care	Consumer
3M	Office Products	Consumer/Business
General Mills	Food	Consumer
Fruit of the Loom	Clothing	Consumer
Philip Morris	Food	Consumer
Loblaws	Retail Food	Consumer
Toys R Us	Retail-Children's	Consumer
Starbucks	Coffee	Consumer

a "bridge-too-far," given the very different nature of this market. Non-alcohol beers compete with many non-beer alternatives. But the company applies this logic to beer markets as well. For example, in the super premium beer segment Philip Morris pushes Lowenbrau, not Miller, rather than confuse the marketplace.

Philip Morris has a fine track record of extending brands—and knowing when to stop. It has kept its Oscar Mayer pork- and beef-based sliced meat brand (for bologna, etc.) separate from its Louis Rich brand of *poultry*-based meat slices. When it went upscale in coffee markets, it did so not with its Maxwell House label but rather launched General Food International Coffees. It extended its Jell-O brand to puddings and frozen pudding confections but did not take it into whipped toppings, where it keeps it Cool Whip brand quite separate.

Knowing how far to extend brands to keep growing clearly calls for good market research that firms such as Philip Morris are skilled at doing. The company extensively tested the caffeine-reduced ground coffee concept for Maxwell House Lite before finally introducing it in

Case 8

A World-Beating Brand Extender: The Story of Fruit of the Loom

Few companies can boast the tremendous sales and profit growth record of Fruit of the Loom, Inc. Since 1987, its sales have doubled to more than $1.8 billion (1993) and its net earnings have more than tripled to $200 million, despite the recessionary economies in which it competes. In 1992, Fruit of the Loom produced over one billion garments, four for every man, woman and child in the U.S., and it still could not satisfy demand. Part of the company's growth has come from its global strategy, which has its sales in Europe growing by 43 percent per year; but a great deal of growth has come from product line extensions into new product categories with the same Fruit of the Loom brand identity.

The company began in underwear and extended its brands into two much larger categories of clothing: active wear and casual wear. Fruit of the Loom active wear includes T-shirts, sweatshirts, turtlenecks, sweatpants, and gym shorts—more than a billion dollars of Fruit of the Loom's total sales. In 1991, the company launched into casual wear, with knitted long pants, casual shorts, and more upscale colored T-shirts for families, but especially women. Both of these product lines provided strong help in the sale of its underwear to mass merchandisers such as Kmart and Wal-Mart, as well as Wholesale Clubs such as Sams.

By extending its lines, Fruit of the Loom has become a much stronger, more critical supplier to these chain stores. Recently Fruit of the Loom has launched Fruit of the Loom bras as part of a joint venture with Warnaco, which manufactures them. In 1991, Fruit of the Loom extended its brand franchise into infant and toddler wear products, including infant underwear called "Fruit of the Loom Baby Style," a new one-piece garment and slip-on shirt decorated in colors, prints, and cartoon characters. As Fruit of the Loom has entered new categories, it has increased the average margins of its sales, since both active wear and casual wear carry far better margins than its traditional underwear. Gross margins increased by 15 percent per year as its sales mix shifted, accounting for a much larger increase in its profit to sales growth rate.

the U.S. Firms less skilled in market understanding often stumble with failed line extensions, such as Cadillac's Cimarron and Life Saver's gum.

Brand Extensions at Retail

As the battle for shelf space has continued between manufacturers' branded products and retailers that have their own store brands, it has become clear that brand extension strategies for retailers also work. Loblaws in Canada has a line of private-label products branded "President's Choice." This brand is not only highly successful—its President's Choice Chocolate Chip Cookies are Canada's top sellers—it has been extended from paper products to peanuts, cola, frozen foods and even beer. It has more than 1,000 "President's Choice" products selling $65 million annually (1993).

Toys R Us, the giant retailer that dominates U.S. retail toy sales, has set up a new book section in its stores called "Books R Us," with children's books provided by its alliance partner Western Publishing, the publisher of "Little Golden" books for kids. Toys R Us may greatly expand its sales of children's books through its 451 stores, with this "store brand" extension of its name for one of its newest departments. Anticipated book sales in 1993–94 are $200 million, which should take a good share of the billion dollar U.S. market.[5] In a similar move in the retail children's apparel market, The Gap has extended its retail brand franchise to children with "Gap for Kids" stores.

Starbucks Coffee Company began in 1971 as a distributor and retailer with its branded presence only attached to whole coffee beans. Now, growing at more than 80 percent annually in sales since 1987, the Starbucks store brand has been extended to fresh-brewed coffee and cappuccino in more than 160 stores. With an extended brand franchise Starbucks bolstered gross profits greatly, since liquid coffee margins exceed raw bean gross margins by 5 to 10 percent.

Merchandising and Bundling Line Assortments

Another platform for sales and profit growth is to increase product variety within a brand's category or to cleverly organize or group products in a way that "out-merchandises" rivals.

Consider 3M's Post-it Note line of sticky notes for offices. 3M could have chosen to license this brand or extend it onto a wide variety of other products. Instead it looked at its Post-It Brand franchise and, taking a leaf from the book of greeting card manufacturers, dreamed up ways to "add value" to paper, with greater Post-It pad variety. It initially innovated in five ways before jumping into new office categories: by adding different sizes of pads; by adding extra colors beyond the original pale yellow color; by producing pads in varying thicknesses; by coming up with pre-printed pads (for instance for phone messages); and by improving the variety and types of Post-It Notes dispensers. Later 3M launched Post-It Tape Flags, Fax Notes, Post-It Flip Charts and Post-It Notes with funny sayings and characters for household use—market extensions of a very different kind.

All of 3M's initial success came from assortment expansion. This assortment expansion allowed it to dominate the category with a blistering array of spin-offs and thereby pre-empt and shut out competitors such as Avery-Dennison. Assortment breadth, when launched by the product pioneer in lightning time, can shut out competitors and enable the pioneer to keep the market lead for many years. Sony's more than 60 models of Walkman and its category dominance attest to the value of assortment breadth.

Flexibility from Assortment Breadth

When firms cover the range of sizes, or quality specs for their product categories, they can prove highly flexible in changing times.

North Word Press is a publisher of nature books. In the mid-1980s it sold books such as *Loon Magic* for $40. But when the 1989–90 recession hit, the sales of high-priced books slumped. So North Word Press developed a lower-cost line of nature books (and added calendars) in the $9.95 range. Gift store bookstore owners liked the books and suggested that some titles in the $19.95 range might also sell. Since 1989 North Word's sales have grown by 22 percent per year to more than $6 million as its good, better, best strategy was put in place and took off. Today, while it sells only very few $40 to $50 books, its mid- and lower-range books continue to sell well, reflecting the more value-conscious consumers of the 1990s.[6]

Full-Line Selling and Product Bundling

Quite apart from allowing for flexible consumer positioning, broad assortment strategies also allow for full-line deal-making to trade channels. Philip Morris gives additional merchandising allowances to more than 200,000 cigarette retailers that stock not only its name-branded cigarettes (Marlboro, Merit, Benson & Hedges) but also its generic unadvertised brands (Basic, Best Buy, and Genco). In exchange for full-line rebates, retailers give Philip Morris more detailed, store-level account information on inventory movement and store promotion plans. The goal of this assortment-bundling program, "Retail Masters," is to get more shelf space for Philip Morris' least popular brands. It is scheduled to run for the three-year 1992–95 period. Without full-line assortment breadth these sorts of programs to secure precious retail shelf space cannot work. Another example is Clorox Company, which leads in ten different U.S. household cleaning categories and is second in four others, due to its full-line approach to bleaches, stain removers, pre-wash cleaners, and toilet bowl lines.

Assortment Combinations: A Growth Differentiator

Duracell International, Inc., the $1.8 billion powerhouse in batteries, has 79 percent share of the U.S. market for consumer alkaline batteries. While it is working on many new products and product applications, such as long-lasting rechargeables for laptop computers and camcorders, the company is facing the problem faced by all market leaders: its growth is slowing down. One growth strategy it relies on is developing new combinations of products and product applications. The battery-tester pack is an example. In 1992, market research had shown that consumers want more than a freshness date on their batteries. They want to *know* that a battery is fresh. The result, Duracell's new combination battery-tester pack, grew sales 7 percent in 1992–93, when overall market growth was at 5 percent.

Outmerchandising rivals with novel product assortments can be a very compelling growth strategy. This is one of the key strategies currently being pursued by computer companies seeking to bundle the sale of their hardware with software and services as a packaged network. International Computers Ltd. PLC of the U.K. has been successful with this assortment strategy. In 1987, it made only 30 percent of its sales, including services or software, but by 1992 this ratio was up to 50 percent. As a result, its sales outpaced other European computer firms and reached $4 billion in 1992. As a basis for comparison, consider another mainframe producer IBM, whose sales of branded software/services were only 36 percent of total sales.

High Product-Assortment/Variety Strategies: The Dangers of Diversity

Filling assortment gaps can also fill market need gaps; and merchandising them well can often increase retail shelf space for a firm's lines.

But there are inherent dangers in variety. Too much variety can add costs in warehousing and manufacturing since among the fast movers, there will always be some "dogs." Wider lines often mean added complexity in production and can spell problems in workforce, machine, and layout productivity.

The best approach, of course, is to offer as much external variety as possible while minimizing internal manufacturing and product handling complexity. Finding the right balance is not an easy matter, though it's not impossible. Honda has modularized its product design components and simplified handling procedures. In European car assembly plants, where modular design has not been well adapted, workers tried to customize on lines designed for mass assembly with disastrous results in costs and productivity. Honda has found a way to standardize variety while many of its European competitors have not, and so the Europeans are suffering higher costs to produce their variety of car models.[7]

There are different approaches to solving the "car makers' riddle" of optimum product variety. One approach is to work backwards in the process and to work closely with suppliers. Many times, their tighter focus on a specific point in the process enables them to more efficiently assemble (subassemble) large components at lower cost. This allows manufacturers to concentrate on the more standardized, primary assembly operations. For instance, Magna is a giant Canadian auto parts subassembler which makes complete door and other larger, complex assemblies in a variety of configurations. As a result the car companies can concentrate on primary assembly of these larger components. In Chrysler's new Intrepid, ten major sections comprise the car, 7 of which are preassembled by outside vendors for Chrysler. (The other three are made by Chrysler itself.) For instance, Textron made the complete dashboard assembly, including the speedometer, radio, air conditioning louvers, glove box door and all plastic facings.

The Growth Masters—Assortments

Company	***Product***	***Market***
3M	Office Products	Consumer/Business
North Word Press	Publishing	Consumer
Philip Morris	Cigarettes	Business
Duracell International	Batteries	Consumer
International Computers Ltd. PLC	Computers	Business
Honda	Automobiles	Consumer
Magna	Auto Parts	Business

Another way to solve the variety dilemma is to add the variety *after* assembly or manufacture. For instance, auto dealers now arrange for a wide variety of accessories and services from rust proofing to installing automotive graphics, different wheel designs, trunk racks, and sun roofs. This allows customers to buy cars suited to their individual tastes and to avoid the problem of managing this universe of tastes or having to guess at customer tastes.

Summary

A solid brand franchise or product design represents a valuable corporate asset. Asset maximization is often achieved by extending the brand to complimentary lines, by licensing it to others, or by augmenting its assortment variety to widen its appeal. Firms looking for growth who attempt to expand users or usage, new products, or taking market share should never neglect the potential of their current line offerings. These may represent great platforms for growth if they can be assorted, merchandised, or extended well. Licensing, flanker branding, and assortment extensions represent three variants on this theme. The next chapter delves even further into this by examining how an improved "services envelope" surrounding a product's sale can boost growth.

Notes

1. Tom Soter, "At the Movies: Marketing Lessons from Tinseltown," *Management Reviews,* Nov. 1992: 10.
2. Robert Hartlein, "Sanyo-Burberry's Announce Licensing Pact," *Women's Wear Daily,* Oct. 14, 1992: 15.
3. *The Economist,* Dec. 26, 1992/Jan. 8, 1993: 98. "The Luxury Goods Trade," by the editors.
4. K. Kelly and K. Miller, "The Rumble Heard Round the World: Harleys," *Business Week,* May 24, 1993: 60.
5. *New York Times News,* Sept. 28, 1992: C6. "Toys R Us's Western Publishing Form Joint Venture."
6. Susan Greco, "Recession Proof Pricing," *Inc.,* April 1993: 27.
7. P. Child, R. Diederich, F.H. Sanders, and S. Wisniowski, "The Management of Complexity," *Sloan Management Review,* Fall 1991: 74.

Chapter 5

Growing Through Services

Augmenting the Sale; Turn-Key Services; Value-Added Services

It matters not whether a company creates . . . a computer, a toaster, or a machine tool, or something you can only experience, such as insurance coverage, an airplane ride, or a telephone call. What counts most is the service built into that something—the way the product is designed and delivered, billed and handled, explained and installed, repaired and received.

Ronald Henkoff
Fortune
"Service Is Everybody's Business"
June 27, 1994, p. 48

It costs much more to sell something to a new customer than to an existing one. Why? There's less risk for the customer. An existing customer already knows your reliability and quality. The important point of this well-known marketing aphorism is: Customers are assets whose potential should not be overlooked and should be maximized to the fullest. The strategies in this chapter—augmentation, turn-key services, and value-added selling—are relatively easy ways to achieve greater profitable growth. Each in its own way enables you to give your customers greater speed, greater efficiency, greater savings, and greater convenience—all of which translate into greater profitability for them and for you.

Surrounding the Sale with Services

If a company can surround its sales with enhanced services before, during, and after the transaction, it will outgrow competitors who don't.

Consider a retailer and the retail sale transaction. There are all sorts of ways to enhance a retail sale and thereby encourage a repeat sale. For instance, prior to a customer's product selection, the retail salesperson can enhance the service by asking questions: Has the customer ever used the product? How does the customer intend to use it? How frequently? And so on. Asking these kinds of questions can help the clerk suggest the product that will best meet—and thereby best satisfy—the customer's needs. The salesperson should be able to clearly explain each product's features and contrast them for the customer. Such information normally includes the product's price and warranty and how the customer can obtain maximum value. This kind of professionalism and courtesy enhances the entire process.

At the sale desk itself, a good retail salesperson explains the different payment options available, makes sure that the product is working properly, and gives the customer service-related information in the event there are any problems later. A good retail salesperson calls the customer the next day to make sure that everything is to the customer's satisfaction.

All of these "services *visibly* demonstrate to a retail customer that his or her business matters to the store. This kind of service is quite separate from the enhancements the store management can make to the sales process. Good signage, dynamic point-of-sale materials, adequate lighting, comfortable dressing rooms, and so forth are important, but they aren't what provide the "service edge." The reason that Nordstroms and Home Depot are outgrowing rivals is because they do these things far better than their competitors. Their services surrounding sales are courteous, prompt, knowledgeable, caring and reliable follow-up—a potent combination that inevitably boosts growth.

The Many Variations of Enhanced Services

While Home Depot can boost its customer service by relying on and enhancing the knowledgeability of its sales staff, many variations on service enhancements are possible. For instance, Sopad Nestlé in France, in order to differentiate its baby food products from Gerber (its biggest competitor), offers a toll-free phone number 10 hours per day for mothers to call and get nutritional advice about babies from licensed dietitians. This service operates six days a week. In addition, Sopad has built way stations along major highways in France so traveling parents can tend to baby changing and feeding needs. The results of these service enhancements? Nestlé's share of the French baby food market went from 20 percent (prior to the service offerings) to 30 percent in the late 1980s and early 1990s—outdistancing Gerber.[2]

Case 9

Home Depot: Enhanced Service in Action

Home Depot has grown from a company of just 10 stores in 2 states with a little more than $100 million in sales (1982) into a major retail powerhouse with sales exceeding $5 billion through more than 175 stores located in 15 states. The company's net earnings per year have grown at a 70 percent compounded rate in the 10-year period from 1982 to 1992. On every financial ratio that counts, Home Depot is a growth-mastering company. How did it do this? Its retail formula is simple, combining three elements: everyday low pricing, large merchandise assortment, and, its biggest single differentiator, customer service. Its target market, do-it-yourselfers, requires a great deal of guidance in the selection of products for home improvement projects.

Home Depot does what many home building retailers do not: it hires and motivates its retail salespersons, mostly ex-tradespersons—carpenters, electricians, plumbers, and the like—to help do-it-yourselfers as nobody else in the industry does. Home Depot hires highly experienced tradesmen and gives them the opportunity to "ply" their trades in an environment that is much more secure than the notoriously unstable construction industry. These individuals have real skill and show affinity for helping by providing expert advice to those less experienced at various types of do-it-yourself projects. Home Depot offers them job stability, generous benefits, and in return these salespeople/ex-tradespeople have proven to be tremendously good at customer service. Once they begin working for Home Depot, most do not return to construction jobs even when they are available.

The company encourages entrepreneurship among its employees and store managers to avoid strait-jacketing these valuable employees in regimented jobs—something so typical of chain stores. Its management structure is highly decentralized, and its pay plans for employees have ample "incentives," including stock purchase plans. The company even encourages its salespeople to stay "on top" of their expertise by also servicing professional repair contractors, which Home Depot also attracts with its bend of professional grade supplies and tools. More than 20 percent of an average Home Depot Store's sales are to professional contractors.[1]

Air Products and Chemicals, a major U.S. producer of industrial gases and chemicals, uses enhanced services to help small accounts grow. (Large accounts already get special account team attention). Small accounts can call a toll-free 800 number for advice from an inside telemarketing rep who, with the assistance of an "expert" system, helps the account to identify which products will match the caller's needs. Then, within 48 hours, Air Products will ship the sample product and accompanying usage information to the prospective customer. If the sample looks good, the customer calls back and Air Products processes the order.

This imaginative service has turned a problem—providing good service to small-volume accounts—into profits. Prior to its expert telemarketing program, small accounts had a difficult time getting through to Air Products' research and development people for answers or guidance because these people usually weren't available. The expert system has captured and systematized the "know-how" of the research and development staff and put it on a database available to telemarketing reps. The enhanced service has helped Air Products greatly penetrate the small account segment of its market in a profitable way.[3]

Milliken and Company, the textile manufacturer, has grown by enhancing the sale of mundane products, such as industrial towels, to laundries. When a laundry buys towels from Milliken, it also gets a computerized routing program that helps the laundry's delivery people efficiently service *their* industrial accounts. (Industrial accounts rent towels to clean tools and equipment). Milliken's program maps out for laundry drivers the most efficient routes to take through a given city to make all the needed pick-ups and deliveries. The company also equips its clients with software to assist them in managing sales leads, inventories, and expenses. In addition, Milliken provides laundries with market research (at no charge) and trains laundry sales representatives. These enhanced services help the laundries with *their* customers and in return Milliken gets a 10 percent price premium over competitors.

How does Milliken keep its customer laundries from accepting its software and training services and then switching to a lower-priced towel supplier? It asks laundries to sign five-year contracts specifying how many towels the laundry will buy during the period. When the five-year contract expires, most laundries re-sign because Milliken keeps improving and upgrading its software and training and the laundries do not want to lose these value-added services.

Milliken demonstrates that services to enhance product sales can be aimed at trade customers and resellers, not just at end users. Sometimes failure to enhance a product's sale in an augmented way can spell disaster. Encyclopedia Britannica failed to enhance its encyclopedia by making it available on CD ROM, and has seen sales plunge with market share moving to its rivals who did this (Compton's Interactive Encyclopedia, Groliers, and Encarta from Funk and Wagnall). Resellers' needs vary quite a lot from needs of end consumers, but when services enhance products sold to them, they can greatly influence growth.

Trade Service Enhancements

Services offered to retailers vary a great deal by the nature of the retailer. For instance, Comp USA, the largest computer retailing superstore chain in the U.S., asks its suppliers to meet its needs on four dimensions:

1. It wants to make a profit on all computers sold and will not work with any computer company offering products it cannot resell at a sufficient gross margin.

2. It must have assured supply from computer makers—this in a business notorious for shortages on new products. Manufacturers won't get Comp USA's business if they cannot provide ongoing stable product availability.
3. It demands just-in-time delivery service to its stores, since it does not have a warehouse, and deals directly with computer manufacturers, not with distributors.
4. It wants access to cooperative advertising funds since it spends in excess of $83 million per year (a sizable percentage of its 827 million dollars in 1992 sales) in advertising suppliers' products.

Comp USA is an excellent example of a firm growing in double digits (52 percent per year in 1992) that knows what services it needs from suppliers and refuses to buy from those that cannot meet its service needs.[4]

Making a reseller's life easier is obviously one way to help your sales to them grow. Leegin Creative Leather Products of Industry, California, proves this maxim.[5] Leegin, which makes leather belts for specialty retailers of casual apparel, grew its sales from $10 million in 1987 to $47 million (almost five times) in 1992 by helping its retailers better understand the merchandising of their belts. Leegin's reps carry laptop computers that can spew out all sorts of data on the store's belt sales including: year-to-date sales versus prior year's sales by belt style, color, and length; belt sales per square foot of space; and belt sales by the newness of styles, helping the retailer determine how new stock is turning. Armed with this data, Leegin's sales reps can advise storeowners on hot and cold sellers. They can suggest optimum mix assortments by length, as well as how much inventory per belt ought to be carried in-store on a monthly basis to prevent stock-outs

The Growth Masters—Augmenting the Sale

Company	*Product*	*Market*
Home Depot	Retail Building Supply	Consumer/Business
Sopad Nestlé	Food	Consumer
Air Products and Chemicals	Chemicals and Gases	Business
Milliken and Company	Textiles	Business
Comp USA	Computers	Consumer/Business
Leegin Creative Leather Products	Clothing	Consumer/Business

(and therefore missed sales). As one of Leegin's accounts has said, "Thanks to them [Leegin], we make a lot of money in the small space we use for belts. It's probably one of our most profitable centers in the store."

Opportunities to leverage growth through service enhancements to retailers abound. JIMCO Furniture Company, a maker of lamps, helped its furniture store customers redesign their displays to offer 56 lamp bases and 72 shades inside a pre-set 12-foot display. Its display was far better organized than most of its competitors' displays, which only allowed a limited selection of 8 to 12 lamps in a 12-foot space. The display, which used a mix-match technique for shades and bases, helped retailers improve inventory turnover and profit margins with no additional space investment, greatly enhancing JIMCO's market share growth in the industry.

Turn-Key Services

One step beyond enhancing a product's sale with services is the notion of assuming the complete management of customers' needs in an area. This could involve allowing a customer to outsource some valued service it currently performs itself, such as its legal services, in-plant printing or data processing. For instance, Johnson Controls, an old-line (founded in 1881) manufacturer of thermostats and controls, now has a separate, fast-growing division that manages the lighting, heating, and security systems of its customers' facilities. Similarly, Xerox assists its customers by assuming the facilities' management of document-processing areas, freeing up a company's own resources from these in-plant printing and copying activities. Similarly, IBM provides facilities management to firms such as Kodak, for which it manages the company's mainframe computer-processing function at Kodak's Rochester, New York, headquarters. On the other end of its operations, in July 1993, IBM gave General Electric Appliances sole right to handle the complete distribution (warehousing, delivery) of IBM personal computer lines to U.S. retailers, such as Wal-Mart, Sears, Office Depot, Circuit City, and Micro Center.

Providing turn-key services of this kind can rapidly grow a firm's sales. Systems and Computer Technology Company (SCT) of Malvern, Pennsylvania, has grown to $91 million in sales by managing the data-processing operations of municipalities, banks, and universities. SCT has a seven-year contract to provide $35 million in outsourced data-processing management (software, networks management, etc.) to Dallas County, Texas. Electronic Data Systems (the firm founded by Ross Perot and now part of General Motors) is an $8 billion colossus built on outsourced business, but firms such as SCT are proving nimble niche competitors. By offering turn-key data processing services to George Washington University, SCT was able to cut the university's staff and $7 million mainframe budget to $4 million by using special customer software and a $500,000 Sequent Computer (versus a $4 million IBM mainframe). The system not only saved the University money (in a tight funding year!) but it also provided professor/administrators with on-line access to student information, class schedules, and other key data via desktop computer.[6]

Two worldwide success stories owe much of their recent growth to their outsourcing turn-key services. One of these is Federal Express. Federal Express' original vision for its business was to "change the way America does business" by making overnight freight services and letter carrying a reality. Having done so, Federal Express altered its vision to "becoming the clipper ship of the information age," taking its services overseas into foreign markets.

Today, the company has a new vision: "to become the logistics arm of the world's economic revolution." Federal Express is becoming a turn-key supplier of logistics services, order processing, warehousing, delivery, shipment tracking, etc., to world-class partners, such as National Semiconductor, Sharp Electronics, Landmark Systems, L.L. Bean (on catalogs) and retailers such as Laura Ashley PLC of England. For example, in a $265 million pact with Laura Ashley, Federal Express will operate a world distribution center in Wales and supply all 500 of Laura Ashley's stores in 28 nations with 24- to 48-hour assured delivery. Federal Express has used this "turn-key" growth strategy to extend its traditional business into new logistics management arenas. For example, it set up a warehouse for National Semiconductor in Singapore to process and ship all of the company's orders worldwide for a 10-year period. The contract for these services is $500 million.[7]

Turn-Key Services: Customer Appeal

While Federal Express provides turn-key services, one could think that this growth strategy platform is mostly the purview of technology service providers, such as Systems and Computer Technology or Electronic Data Systems. Not so.

Baxter Healthcare division of Baxter International has grown very rapidly as the leading supplier of healthcare product systems and

Exhibit 5–1
The Evolution of Federal Express' Business Vision

The Vision Statement	The Business
• Original (1970s): "Changing the Way America Does Business"	• Overnight Delivery Service (U.S.)
• Evolved (1980s) into: "Become the Clipper Ship of the Information Age"	• Delivery service worldwide
• Evolved (1990s) into: "Become the Logistics Arm of the World's Economic Revolution"	• Management of entire logistics systems (not just delivery) on a global basis for global companies

services through turn-key management of hospital inventories. Baxter reengineered itself into a single-source supplier of hospital supplies by offering hospitals the ability to outsource the inventory management of a great range (120,000) of products. Baxter provides hospitals with stockless inventory control, warehousing services, and even recycling programs (for products such as intravenous bags and bottles), activities that formerly cost hospitals space, time, and money.

Baxter's network of 120 worldwide warehouses supplies hospitals with a thousand of its own manufactured items, in addition to one thousand of other suppliers products, from soft drinks, to medical/surgical supplies and even bibles. Between 1989 and 1992 alone, Baxter grew from $7.3 billion to more than $9 billion. The company offers hospitals integrated materials management, guaranteed delivery, and extensive reporting on purchases and orders to hospitals.

Baxter's "Value Link" program allows "just-in-time delivered product to individual hospital departments in ready-to-use packages in volumes demanded" (seven days a week).[8] In exchange for such services, hospital customers commit to purchasing the products covered by the system from Baxter on an exclusive partnership basis.

The power of such turn-key logistics services to grow Baxter's sales volume is phenomenal. In just four hospital cases (reported in *Sloan Management Review* from Baxter sources) Baxter gained combined sales of $283 million from five and one-half years of contracts with four hospitals (approximately $12.7 million per hospital per year).

In exchange, these hospitals saved, on a net basis, *annualized* savings of anywhere from $2 million to $3 million due to reduced inventories, purchasing, staffing, storage space, carrying charges, etc.

Turn-key service clearly is not a growth strategy merely for service companies since Baxter manufactures intravenous solution, garments, disposable kits and trays, catheters and tubes, surgical packs, gloves, dialysis supplies, respiratory products, dietary supplies, bandages, prenatal supplies and medical dressings.[9]

The basic reason for the appeal of turn-key services is that savings to the target customer often occur in multiple expense areas. As Exhibit 5–2 illustrates, money is saved in product acquisition costs such as purchasing, expediting, order entry and verification; as well as in-possession costs attached to inventories, such as taxes, insurance, storage, interest, obsolescence, and shrinkage; and usage costs attached to training, maintenance, and labor costs. Baxter saves hospitals money in two of these three areas, acquisition and possession costs, while firms such as SCT save firms costs in acquisition and in usage costs attached to data processing staffing, training, maintenance, and installation. All of these cost savings are usually associated with non-value-adding activities not considered central to a hospital's mission of care or to a university's mission of teaching and research.

The Growth Masters—Turn-Key Services

Company	*Product*	*Market*
Johnson Controls	Facilities Management	Business
Xerox	Office Products	Business
Systems and Computer Technology Company	Computers/Office Systems	Business
Federal Express	Logistics	Business
Baxter Healthcare/ Baxter International	Healthcare	Business
J.B. Hunt Transport Services	Transportation	Business

There is an additional advantage to outsourcing to turn-key service providers. They are experts at what they do because they are focused on doing that specific task and nothing else, so the quality of the services they provide is often higher than a firm's own staff can provide or than can be provided by buying these outside services on a piecemeal, nonintegrated basis. For example, when IBM turned its retail distribution over to General Electric Appliances, it did so because, according to an IBM-Gallup survey of retailers, GE Appliances ranked number one in all categories of delivery-warehouse service. Buying turn-key services from others also allows firms to downsize a noncritical function. J.B. Hunt Transport Services has become America's largest publicly held truckload carrier, moving up from 129th in size several years ago, in no small part due to firms outsourcing fleet services.

Positioning Value-Based Services

A value-based strategy is a truly customer-driven approach to growth, but "value" is only in the eyes of the customer. It is a relative concept.

Exhibit 5–2
Turn-Key Service Providers: The Three Major Cost-Saving Areas

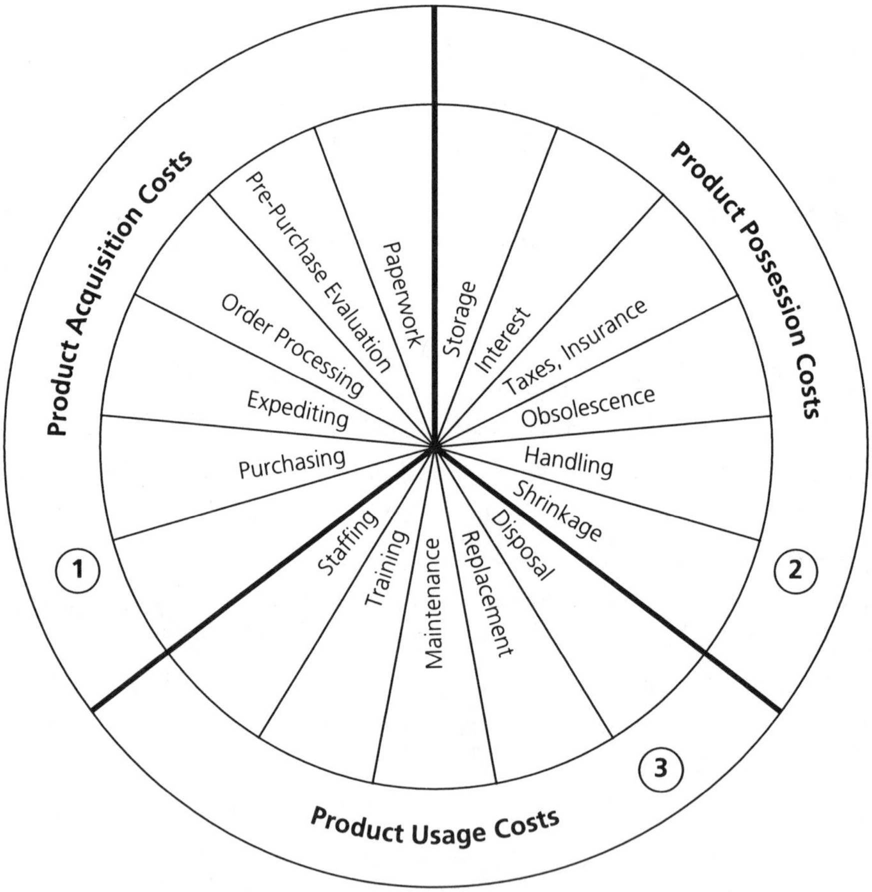

Companies that pursue value positioning usually use one of the following four tactics that enable them to define *value* in concrete, customer-relevant terms and to differentiate themselves from competitors:

- Speed: save customers time by being faster with service than a competitor.
- Savings or "value pricing": be less expensive (while providing the same level of quality) than a key rival.
- Service: offer more comprehensive service that minimizes a customer's worries and ensures that the customer is never let down on a product's availability.
- Simplicity: make the customer's life easier by removing complexity from an otherwise time-consuming service or product. Exhibit 5–3 diagrams these tactical variations on the value-based service theme.

Saving Customers Money

Giving customers more value for identical or similar product quality has near-universal appeal. Such is the appeal of COSTCo Wholesale Corp., a membership club with more than 2.3 million individual members and 1.4 business members. In 1984, its sales to members were just over $100 million, but by 1992 they exceeded $6.5 billion. In 1992 its net *income* of $113 million exceeded 1984 gross revenue of $102 million. CostCo merged with Price Club in 1993 and doubled its size.

How was COSTCo able to grow from 7 warehouses to 89 in less than 10 years? It has a price/value formula that saves customers money on brand name merchandise. As with all membership clubs (including PACE and Sam's), COSTCo has turned the act of saving customers'

Exhibit 5–3
Value-Based Service Differentiators

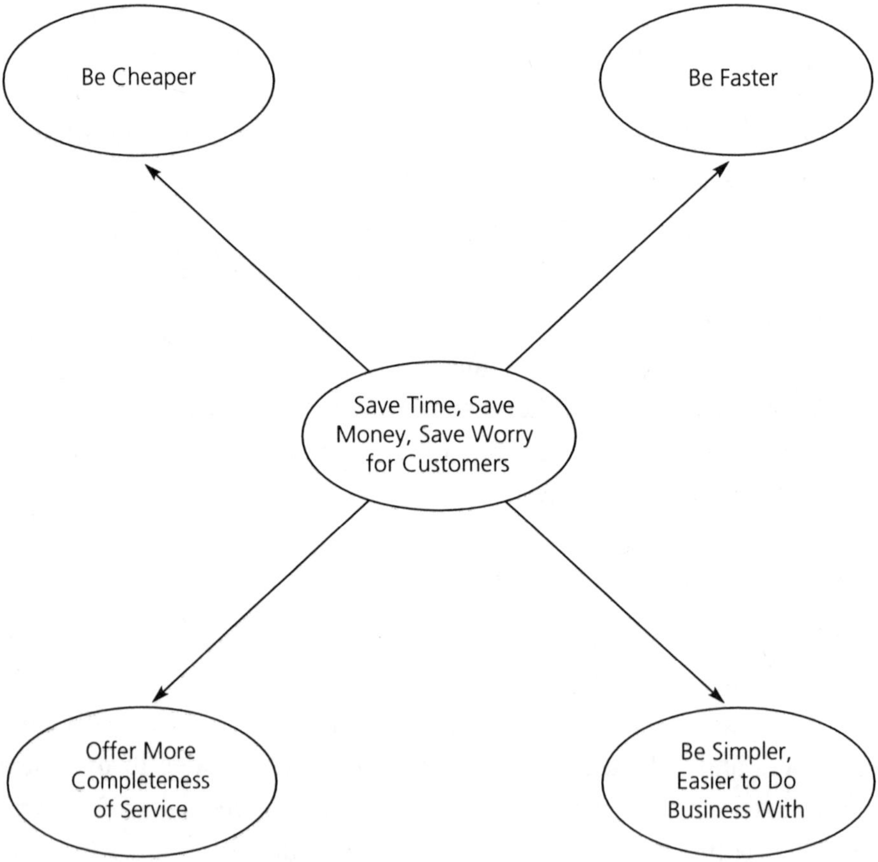

money into an art form by systematically removing costs from traditional retail formulas. In many ways its service to customers has been eliminating services the customer did *not value* and concentrating on those that the customer *did value.* Traditional retail costs it has systematically reduced include:

- In-store fixtures (warehouse environment in lighting, shelving, aisles, paint decor, etc.)
- Store location (non-prime real estate locations, non-mall areas)
- Staffing (minimal on-site shopping assistance)
- Merchandise assortment breadth (narrower assortments, fewer size and flavor variations)
- Advertising (why advertise to nonmembers?)
- Paperwork (hook-up to suppliers via electronic data interchange (E.D.I.) systems)
- Freight (pickup from vendors, demanding significant pickup freight allowances that more than offset their costs)
- Middlemen (buy direct from manufacturers, saving costs in volume buying and margins)
- Bad debts (by screening memberships it minimizes bad check losses)
- Labor costs (its hours of operation are 10 A.M. to 8:30 P.M., shorter than traditional discount, department or grocery retailers).

COSTCo has preserved the following customer services considered important:

- Brand name merchandise

Case 10

Novel Ways of Saving Money: Homecorp

Homecorp, based in Montgomery, Alabama, is an apartment rental company with 14,000 apartments in 65 different communities nationwide. In the apartment rental industry it is very difficult to differentiate yourself based on value. Most rents are similar by accommodation size and furnishings, and it's difficult to make customers feel special in a substantial cost-related way. But Homecorp has found a way. It offers renters a membership in "Home Club," which entitles them to discounts on an array of services from well-known local retailers, entertainment vendors, and service suppliers. Its special discounts cover such well-known firms as Lenscrafters, 800-Flowers, Camelot Music, General Cinema movie tickets, Royal Caribbean Cruise Lines, Ryder Truck Rentals, Sprint Communications, Cort Furniture, and Public Storage.

These discounts have produced very high renewal rates (exceeding industry averages by 25 percent). And the value payoff isn't just to Homecorp's tenants. The company benefits because the higher renewal rates mean less turnover and less maintenance and apartment preparation—every time an apartment changes hands it costs $500 to prepare it for the next tenant. In addition, the discounts have given Homecorp brand name recognition, so that renters who do move away often seek out another Homecorp development in order to keep their Home Club discount membership valid.[10]

- Deep stocks of popular sizes always fresh due to rapid stockturns
- Ample parking with good access to major roads
- Low mark-ups on everyday low prices

Driven by this "cost-reduction obsession" management, warehouse clubs such as COSTCo have struck a new balance between price and service, trading off the value of selling low-priced brand names with the cost of providing a lot of in-store assistance that requires higher prices—and it has done so without eliminating services that customers truly do "value."

The Value of Speed

Another variant on value-based services involves offering a product or service in a way that saves the buyer time in the purchase or acquisition cycle. British Airways has a new mobile airline check-in system designed to shorten passenger waiting times at airport counters. Airline staff carry hand-held computers with built-in software that can tap into the mainframe computers via radio hookup and allow them to provide on-the-spot check-in of lined-up passengers. This system enables staff to secure passengers' boarding passes and luggage reservations without having to wait to reach the main counter terminal check-ins. While this saves customers time, it also helps British Airways since late-departing passengers delayed by other connections cost the company dearly, with 900 pounds of fuel burning per minute in every Boeing 747 kept idling by latecomers. The savings in fuel alone approximates $16 million annually.

In product manufacturing companies, being fast for customers is also a great tactic. Kingston Technology is the fastest growth company on *Inc.* magazine's 1992 Top 500 list (at $230 million in sales and 100 percent growth from 1991 to 1992). Kingston makes memory upgrade products for personal computers but does so, unlike any of its 15 competitors, at lightning speed. The company books, builds, and ships an order for a personal computer memory upgrade on the *same day*—unheard of in its field until Kingston did it! Its customers, such companies as Ingram Micro of Santa Ana, California, and Gates F/A in Greenville, South Carolina, can place orders one day and have delivery to their warehouse the next.

And Kingston doesn't sacrifice product quality because its engineering and technical support staff are the best in its niche of the industry. Owner John Tu sums up its speed value added service by stating: "We want to make it so the customer can't afford *not* to do

The Growth Masters—Value-Based Services

Company	***Product***	***Market***
COSTCo	Warehouse Club	Consumer
Homecorp	Apartment Rental	Consumer
British Airways	Travel/Transportation	Consumer/Business
Kingston Technology	Computers	Business
Premier Industrial Corp.	Industrial Components	Business
Saturn	Automobiles	Consumer

business with us!"[11] Kingston has come a long way since starting with two employees in 1987 (now 130).

Adding value for customers sometimes saves both buyers and sellers money. When a firm offers remote diagnostic service for machinery, whereby it can determine a problem with a customer's machine by telephone or modem, it can save the customer time and money, as well as its own travel costs and time.

Hassle-Free Service

Like the term *value, service* is relative. As warehouse clubs have shown, all services are not equal. But in some industries, customers define service as *completeness* of service—knowing that a product will be available when and where it is needed. A fine example of growing through service completeness is Premier Industrial Corp., a $650 million enterprise that sells 100,000 different industrial parts ranging from electronic components to industrial fasteners, maintenance parts, welding supplies, lubricants, and specialty chemicals. Premier's ace in the hole? Its inventory of all 100,000 items, slow and fast movers alike, is second to none. It tries to never let its 250,000 customers down, always keeping all items—from the hard-to-find to the mundane—in stock. It charges full prices for such service, but its 3,000 salespersons care deeply about customers and will pull all strings to see that customers are satisfied with service completeness.

Even though almost everything Premier makes or sells would normally be labeled a commodity, the company has grown at 9.4 percent compounded annual growth for the last 20 years, and its return on assets is four times its industry average and its earnings-per-share have sustained a 14½ percent growth for more than 25 years.[12] The reason? Its customers know that whatever they need will be available when they need it.

Simplify, Simplify, Simplify

Make it easy. Make the problems go away. Fewer things can win a customer's heart—and business—more quickly and more profitably. And, conversely, few things make customers angrier than haggling over major purchases in ways that play on their insecurities and confusion; yet that is precisely what occurs in a great many car dealerships. Dickering over price annoys more than 68 percent of the car buying public, yet dealers have chosen to ignore such research because *they* don't want to change. J.D. Power & Associates of Agoura Hills, California, best known for its customer satisfaction index of new cars, has recently done research that demonstrates that dealerships with "no dicker pricing" are increasing sales and customer satisfaction faster than traditional dealerships. One-price programs have proven successful and popular at Saturn and Ford dealerships, since customers can concentrate on performance aspects of the automobile rather than on the buying process. This form of value essentially removes complexity from a risky, often anxiety-creating experience and represents a good example of shifting the basis of service differentiation from price to performance.

One outstanding example of the potency of simplicity is illustrated by Intuit, the original developer of Quicken Software. The company grew to more than $228 million in sales in just ten years by making its personal finance software the easiest to use in the world. Most software is about as simple to operate as a spaceship. But not Quicken, which draws raves from users about how it simplifies their lives in writing checks, paying bills, and balancing checkbooks. Quicken's simplicity advantage defeated all competitors' products, including that sold by Microsoft, which acquired Quicken in 1994 for $1 billion.

Summary

Regardless of which service differentiation strategy you use, it will almost undoubtedly involve investment in information technology. Information technology can help match inventories to sales, track customer buying profiles, schedule employees for optimum customer coverage, forecast component demand, or help route delivery vehicles. It is communications technology and computers that drive the expert systems used by Baxter Health Care, British Airways, Homecorp, and the other companies mentioned in this chapter. In Japan, 7-11 Stores replace 2,100 of the 3,000 items carried annually, adjusting them to buyer preferences, all made possible by a $200 million sales and inventory tracking system. Even in a business as ordinary as hair salons, computers are used to match stylist staffing to peak demand times, and to use data about customers for direct mail promotions and coupon drops. If there is one common element that cuts across the three major strategy platforms for growth in this chapter, it is the presence of information and telecommunications technology to fuel augmented, turn-key, and value-added service offerings to customers.

Notes

1. *World Executives Digest,* Feb. 1992: 61. "Offer the Extra Value Proposition," by the editors.
2. Home Depot's *Annual Financial Report,* Feb. 1992: 12.
3. *Index Alliance "Executive Forum,"* Dec. 1991. "Achieving Customer Commitment Through Customer Excellence" by CSC Index Cambridge Center, Cambridge U.S.A. (a private industry newsletter).
4. Joe Mullich, "Comp USA Morton Weds Retail—PC's," *Business Marketing,* June 1993: 26.
5. Quote from Don Zuidema Sporting Club of West Hollywood's owner, quoted in *Inc.* magazine, June 1993: 88. John Case, "A Business Transformed" (a profile of Leegin Creative Leather Products).
6. John Verity, "They Make a Killing Minding Other People's Business," *Business Week,* Nov. 3, 1992: 96.
7. Daniel J. McConville, "Reinventing Fed Ex," *World Trade,* Jan. 1993: 35–38.
8. James Short and N. Venkatraman, "Beyond Business Process Redesign: Redefining Baxter's Business Network," *Sloan Management Review,* Fall 1992: 17. Describes Baxter's integrated logistics services to hospitals in detail.
9. *Health Industry Today,* Feb. 1986: 25. For a list of Baxter's products.
10. Howard Schlossburg, "Home Club Discounts Give Renters a Reason to Stay," *Marketing News,* Feb. 15, 1993: 15.
11. Edward Welles, "Built on Speed," *Inc.,* Oct. 1992: 88.
12. Michael Verespej, "Mort Mandel, C.E.O. of Premier Industrial Corp.," *Industry Week,* Mar. 1, 1993: 23–26.

Chapter 6

Growing Through Collaboration

Acquisitions, Alliances, and Joint Ventures

Why limit productivity advances to what your firm can do alone?

Jordan D. Lewis
Partnerships for Profit

All of the strategies discussed thus far in this book have at least one thing in common. They involve approaches that companies can use to "grow their own" on their own: to achieve profitable growth by building the company's existing assets—its customers, its products and their applications, and its existing relationships in the marketplace. However, sometimes a firm needs to go beyond its current internal strengths. Sometimes it makes sense to "buy" a market through acquisition of an existing firm; and other times collaboration in the form of a strategic alliance or a joint venture makes better sense. Although these can be treacherous waters relative to the other strategies, the growth they bring often more than offsets the risks involved in "running the rapids."

Take the case of R.R. Donnelley and Sons, the world's largest printer. Since 1879, the company has grown to over $4.2 billion in sales and $235 million plus in net profits, as a direct result of both acquisitions and partnerships. Donnelley has bought its way into new segments of printing (such as Metromail—the largest mailing list business in the U.S.) as well as into overseas markets. It bought printers in Ireland, England, Japan, Mexico and Singapore. And to gain entry to mainland Europe it has a printing partnership with Hachette, a giant French publisher.

By going outside its own home-grown growth strategies R.R. Donnelley has grown from $1.4 billion in 1982 to $4.2 billion in 1992, a decade later, almost all by acquisition and partnership. While growing with the kinds of internal activities discussed in previous chapters provides a company tight control and focus, acquisitions, collaborations, and joint ventures involve new or shared risks and control and more often than not require substantial adjustments in a company's fundamental skill sets and know-hows. Depending upon how these riskier growth vectors are pursued, a firm's strengths can be supplemented and further developed *or* can be sapped. Once again, the two key criteria for using these growth avenues are: do they provide *sustainable* growth and is it quality growth, in which top-line revenue expansion is followed in turn by net income growth. In Donnelley's case when sales grew from a little more than $1 billion to over $4 billion, its profits also more than doubled (from $91 million in 1982 to $235 million in 1992).

Acquisitions: Buying Your Way to Growth

Bacardi, makers of Rum, with a strong business in North America, bought Martini and Rossi, whose strong brands and solid European distribution network will help Bacardi move ahead in Europe. Gillette, which owns Papermate Pens, bought Parker Pen Holdings (U.K.) in order to further its share of the global pen business. General Mills, makers of Cheerios, bought RJR/Nabisco's cold cereal brands such as Shredded Wheat, while RJR/Nabisco bought Stella D'Oro Biscuit. America's largest family-owned cookie maker, Nabisco is sixth in breakfast cereal share, so its cereal division was not as strategically important as it was to General Mills. Yet RJR/Nabisco is one of the world leaders in cookies, so its acquisition of Stella D'Oro's lines, which are in the premium-priced end of the cookie market, helps it solidify its position.

Each of these four acquisitions illustrates the dual reasoning behind acquisitions: They occur as firms seek to boost share positions and growth in markets in which they have a strategic stake, and they occur because buying well-known brands via acquisitions can be less expensive than starting new brands from scratch. In consumer products, a single brand can require enormous outlays ($10 million in the U.S.; $20 million globally), not to mention other substantial costs.

An acquisition that fits well with a company's existing product line-up can provide a strong shot in the arm for two reasons. First, it facilitates synergy with existing distribution logistics systems. Second, it provides instant cash flow from the day the brand is acquired. And cash flow is probably the highest hurdle that new consumer products face. Fighting for shelf space in crowded consumer markets is not conducive to prudent financial management. So as the costs of new brand creation and commercialization in consumer markets have escalated, reasonably priced acquisitions have begun to look more attractive as a way to grow.

The key, of course, is the fit of the acquired brands with the firm's own and the price paid to acquire them. For instance, RJR/Nabisco paid only $100 million for Stella D'Oro, a very reasonable price for a premium brand with expansion potential. Similarly, General Foods' acquisition of Shredded Wheat and the other Nabisco cereals was only $450 million for cereals that complement its own brands without overlapping them. Each of these acquisitions passed the test of fit and value.

Make or Buy: The Key Question

Buying assets is often less expensive and risky than building them from scratch. The buyer avoids early start-up costs *and* often can find reasonably priced assets selling at a substantial discount for any number of reasons. Sometimes a property becomes available because its owner considers it a nonstrategic business. Sometimes the property is available because the seller is in financial difficulty and needs cash to stay afloat. Sometimes its owner doesn't have the market strength or management skill to maximize its potential. Consider Thorn EMI PLC, a $6 billion London-based giant in the record business. EMI Music, Thorn's major source of revenue and profit, has owned record labels since 1962, when its Parlophone subsidiary signed the Beatles. EMI lost the knack for finding new recording talent in the seventies and merged with Thorn Electrical Industries in 1979 to avoid bankruptcy.

In the eighties Sir Colin Southgate, Thorn EMI's CEO, set out to alter the company's fortunes by buying record labels rather than trying to find and sign its own talent. Using the proceeds from the sale of some of Thorn's defense and electronics businesses, Southgate bought Chrysalis Records and Virgin Music Group in the U.K. and Sparrow Corp and SBK Records in the U.S. With these labels, he diversified the talent base to include Sinead O'Connor, Janet Jackson, the Rolling Stones, Garth Brooks, and Vanilla Ice. EMI's acquisitions contributed 86 percent of the firm's total profits of $180 million, and it now boasts the world's largest music publishing catalog, with rights to 850,000 songs.

Through strategic acquisitions, EMI has signed artists from all genres of music including rock, rhythm and blues, jazz, country, rap, and even Christian music.[1] And EMI's distribution and administration skills (in royalties, etc.) are now spread across multiple labels, which has made it possible to manage the newly acquired firms at far lower costs than they could be managed as separate entities. It helps, of course, to be a shrewd buyer of talent, as Sir Colin is, as well as an astute negotiator of purchases. EMI will earn back the purchase price of these firms in less than five years, given the firm's worldwide sales.

Multiple Fits

While EMI's acquisition successes fit into a narrow market, as did RJR/Nabisco's and General Mills, a fit to a branded portfolio—buying products that play to the firm's strengths—is only one type of acquisitions strategy. Two other strategies are making acquisitions that extend and exploit a company's core skills and making acquisitions that exploit a firm's customer base.

Case 11

Exploiting Your Customer Base: Newell Company

Newell Company has grown from a $14 million family-owned drapery hardware maker to a $1.1 billion powerhouse of high-volume hardware, housewares, and office products. Its 25 key customers, including firms such as Kmart, Wal-Mart, Target, Ace Hardware, Home Depot, and Office Depot, are in five segments: office superstores, discount stores, warehouse clubs, hardware stores, and home centers. It has grown almost entirely through synergistic acquisitions.

Over the years, Newell has looked to purchase firms that make staple, affordable lines with recognized brand names and solid market shares in categories of products that do not require it to do much advertising. Newell relies on its retailer partners to draw consumers to its brands and concentrates on assisting the retailer with tailored sales programs, merchandising supports, on-time deliveries, and computer-to-computer ordering. Each of these supports allows the retailer to delegate to Newell the management of its products categories that Newell sells; Newell keeps the category inventory current, fast moving, and well displayed. Product categories in which Newell is number one or number two in the market are listed in Exhibit 6–1 with their "brand names."

Newell's strategy of using acquisitions to supply a limited customer base is very much in tune with retailer trends, where consolidation is occurring rapidly. And the financial results of Newell's acquisitions have been outstanding, with a 15-year compounded profit growth of 24.6 percent, compounded sales growth of 19 percent, and an average return on equity of 21 percent. In a retail market where growth has been paltry (3–4 percent) it is today growing its business at 8 percent per year, double the industry rate.

Exhibit 6–1
Newell's Category Coverage

Store Category	Newell Brands
Glassware	Anchor-Hocking
Shelving	Dorfile
Bath Scales	Counsellor
Office Products	Keene
	W.T. Rogers
	Sanford
Hand-Torches	Bernz-o-matic
Cookware/Bakeware	Mirro
	Wear Ever
Cabinet/Window Hardware	Amerock
Paint Applicators	EZ Painter
Window Furnishings	Newell

An excellent example of the former is Minebea, the world's leading producer of miniature ball bearings. With 52 subsidiaries, 30,000 employees, and $2.1 billion in sales, Minebea has grown its business through acquisitions that exploit four key skills: precision machining, hardening metal coatings on small components, skilled electronics management in delicate manufacturing processes, and knowledge of specialized materials and alloys. In 1970 Minebea controlled 70 percent of the world market for miniature ball bearings ranging from 30 millimeters to 3 millimeters in diameter. These bearings are used in electrical equipment and instrumentation.

Recognizing that its share had probably topped out, the company began a series of acquisitions to buy companies that make small motor components, electromagnetic clutches, electric motors, cooling fans, and aircraft propellers—all products that are dependent on small bearings. One such acquisition was Reed Instrument in the U.S. Minebea understood the skill needs of these types of firms, since most of them already were customers of its miniature ball bearings. To further exploit its core skills, Minebea looked to acquire other firms that could use its know-hows even though they didn't use their bearings. To pursue this track the company bought makers of precision gauges, small fasteners, loudspeakers, small transformers, die castings and computer keyboards. Each of these firms utilized Minebea's core skills, and each subsequently has been a big success as part of Minebea's total company. Interestingly, only 28 percent of Minebea's current sales come from miniature bearings, so successful has been its use of these acquisitions to expand from its Japanese base. It is now much more of a global company. In fact, 60 percent of its sales comes from nations outside Japan.[2]

Mergers: Managing a Fragmented Business

If a firm can acquire competitors whose geographic scope does not overlap its own, it can often merge such companies into considerable powerhouses. This occurred in the waste management industry and is occurring in U.S. ambulance services. American Medical Response of Boston has grown to a $94-million ambulance service provider by acquiring four large companies in California, Connecticut, and Delaware and filling in around them with mom and pop ambulance services. The company applies state-of-the-art satellite technology and management to ambulance dispatch to provide a response time of six minutes, far better than the industry average. It plans to grow its sales via acquisition to $300 million by 1995.

Another example of two merged firms forming a more powerful company is Merisel, the $2.3 billion distributor of microcomputers and software, formed from the 1990 union of Softsell (California) and Microamerica (Massachusetts). Since the merger, their combined revenues have doubled, and profits are 73 percent greater.

The Growth Masters—Acquisitions

Company	***Product***	***Market***
R.R. Donnelley and Sons	Printing	Consumer/Business
Bacardi	Beverages	Consumer
General Mills	Food	Consumer
RJR/Nabisco	Food	Consumer
Thorn EMI PLC	Entertainment/Recording	Consumer
Minebea	Industrial Parts	Business
Newell Company	Hardware	Consumer/Business
American Medical Response	Ambulance Services	Consumer/Business
Merisel	Microcomputers	Business
Alco Standard	Office Products	Consumer/Business

Avoiding Unrelated Acquisitions

While Newell, Minebea, and EMI Music have been astute, focused acquisitors, many firms have diversified into a hodge-podge of businesses with minimal relation to their core skills, core customers, or core product lines. Random acquisitions often prove disastrous on three dimensions: the acquiring firm doesn't know how to manage what it has bought because it is such a different business; due to lack of knowledge, the acquiring firm often overpays for the acquired firm and can never get a payback; and without management synergy the acquisition assumes few "value-added" dimensions in its new form.

Alco Standard, a highly skilled $4.9 billion conglomerate that acquired more than 300 companies from 1965 to 1986, learned through hard-won experience the problems of random acquisition. The company has sold off a myriad of firms, keeping only those in two major businesses, office products and paper distribution. These two divisions are all that remains of the nine Alco Standard divisions that existed in 1986. It sold off divisions in such diverse fields as ice cream, coal mining, health services, motor homes, electronic scoreboards, food services equipment, and liquor distribution. And as it has pared back its focus, its financial returns have improved. Its five-year return on equity is 15 percent, and $100 invested in Alco Standard's stock in 1965 has compounded at 19 percent and is now worth $11,000. The last three CEO's of Kodak have spent considerable time and energy divesting the company of ill-starred acquisitions. So making the wrong acquisitions can chew up a lot of management attention—not just in trying to make them work but also in eventually closing them down or selling them off.

Sensibly focused acquisitions done by smart operators like Newell, Alco Standard, or Thorn EMI can pay off, but buying companies requires skills in one than just financial manipulation. Acquisitions for growth require a firm to merge the human balance sheets of their companies, that is, the processes and cultures of both companies. Obviously, the risks are considerably more manageable when the companies share common knowledge of their markets, technologies, or customers. Most successful acquirers appear to use the marketing strategy of "segment, concentrate, and dominate," whether doing so by brand (Gillette), by technology (Minebea), or by customer market linkage (Alco Standard and Newell).

Alliances with Other Firms

Because acquisitions can be turbulent and risky for both the acquired and acquirer, a great many companies are choosing a less perilous approach to growth through combination: doing business jointly in an alliance. An alliance is an informal collaboration between firms that does not involve the setup of a joint-venture company or the outright purchase of one firm by another. Instead, the companies simply agree to take some tangible aspect of mutual interest to them—a market, technology, a product, a factory, etc.—and share in its development or exploitation.

There are any number of obvious reasons for this kind of collaboration. Basically, each firm may control an asset that the other wants to share, and forming an alliance enables both parties to benefit with a minimum amount of formal structure. For example, Merck, a giant in the pharmaceutical business, spun off some of its smaller drugs into an alliance with DuPont, a small player in the market. DuPont needed to expand its line so that its small sales force would have more products to sell to physicians; Merck, on the other hand, needed a partner who would help it exploit drug sales opportunities in categories too small to interest its own large sales force, which was aggressively selling its new drugs in markets with larger sales potential. Each brought an asset into the collaboration—DuPont a small well-focused sales force and Merck new small-scale drugs—for mutual gain. DuPont pays Merck a royalty on sales, while keeping the balance of sales and profits.

The reason for alliances often tends to vary with the industry. At the University of Limburg's (Holland) Maastricht Economic Research Institute, some 4,182 alliances were studied in 15 separate industries from high tech, such as computers and robotics, to large equipment manufacturers in defense, aerospace, or automotive markets, as well as in new fields of science such as biotechnology or new materials. Researchers have discovered that alliances are formed for four major reasons.

1. Alliances allow markets to be accessed or developed more readily. When Nestlé acquired Jardine's Dairy Farm, it gained control of Jardine's, which had an ice cream plant in Guangzhou, China. The Chinese appetite for Western-style ice cream is growing, and Nestlé gained instant access to this market.
2. Alliances allow for just-in-time exploitation of technology that would otherwise take a firm too long to develop by itself (in biotechnology, or microelectronics, for instance).
3. Alliances enable the development of projects that are too costly or risky for a single company to develop alone (such as the Airbus consortium that developed the Airbus to compete with Boeing's 747).
4. Alliances allow for product or market gap filling products to emerge as partners share complimentary know-hows, such as Apple Computer's alliance with Sony, which built Apple's successful "Powerbook" laptop computer. Collaboration brings together firms whose shared skills can help each leapfrog competition with new products that plug holes in the market.

Firms seeking partners to share assets, skills, markets or new product initiatives, often are competitors in parts of the market outside the framework of the alliance. IBM and Apple are allied in software development but compete in personal computers. Toyota and General Motors compete in selling cars, while collaborating in manufacturing them. Coca-Cola competes with Cadbury Schweppes for end consumer preference, yet in the U.K. their distribution alliance has helped both grow market share, Coca-Cola in colas and Schweppes in ginger ales. Pilkington Glass has formed alliances in markets such as auto glass, where its presence is not strong, with Nippon Sheet Glass and Saint-Gobain, its rivals in other glass markets. Alliances for growth are very much driven by the potential of the specific opportunity rather than the niceties of competitive rivalry.

Alliances Prompted by Industry Turmoil

Occasionally an industry will face upheaval in the traditional dynamics that have sustained it. This is occurring in the pharmaceutical industry, where for many years drug makers enjoyed fat profits and regular, unchallenged price hikes for their products. As health care reform threatens these practices, international drug firms are seeking alliances to tap different parts of the industry's profit stream:

1. Merck bought Medco, a mail order drug company that also advises doctors on how to prescribe less expensively. Medco pioneered "pharmacy-benefit" management.
2. Eli Lilly is buying PCS Health Systems, Inc., the largest managed health care company in the United States. PCS manages health care plans for 50 million people.
3. France's Rhone Poulenc Rorer, Pfizer, and Bristol Myers Squibb of the U.S. have formed an alliance with Caremark, a Medco rival.

4. SmithKline Beecham purchased Diversified Pharmaceutical Services.

The result of these huge alliances is that the drugs of 90 percent of the U.S. population will be covered by one of the companies mentioned above—effectively putting all of the large drug firms in the business of managed benefit plans. These firms, which grew enormously from new scientific discoveries, clearly intend to diversify their businesses into new, more profitable areas in an era of restricted pricing and generic prescriptions.

Multiplayer Alliances

While the majority of alliances are between two companies, many involve consortiums. Alliances allow companies to reconcile the gap between their ambitions to exploit markets, technologies, factories, distribution systems, brands, or patents with their financial, geographic, technological, or functional resources. For example, in developing a new super jumbo jet, Boeing is collaborating with two competitors, McDonnell Douglas and Airbus, as well as other key component manufacturers, Mitsubishi, Kawasaki, and Fuji.[3] IBM's personal computer was developed by a collaborative alliance with Microsoft, Intel, and Lotus.

Telecommunications giants in the U.S. such as Bell Atlantic have been able to grow overseas almost entirely by alliances with European, Asian, or South Pacific companies. Recognizing that its growth in the U.S. would be restricted to six mid-Atlantic states and the District of Columbia, it made major efforts to form overseas alliances. Its alliance partners consist of CGI in France; Telefonica in Spain; Czech and Slovak Posts and Telecommunications in Czechoslovakia; Norvans in Norway; PTT Telecom in Holland; Korea Telecommunications Authority in South Korea; and DGT in Taiwan. Alliances such as these often allow firms to "hedge their bets" about future technologies that may—or may not—catch on. By forming an alliance and loaning resources to alliance partners in emerging technologies, the company can keep an eye on the technologies development at a low entry cost. Sony has several U.S.-based technology alliances in video-conferencing (with Panavision), computer storage (with Exabyte), and high definition television (with Compression Labs).

Alliances Prompted by Trade Pacts

Trade pacts invariably spawn cross-border alliances. For example, when the North American Free Trade Agreement (NAFTA) was signed by Canada, the U.S., and Mexico, the beer industry began forming continental alliances. Miller Brewing bought a 20 percent position in Molson Breweries of Canada, and Anheuser Busch bought 18 percent of Mexico's Grupo Modello, makers of Corona Beer. And in July 1994, John Labatt, Canada's second largest brewer, allied with Mexico's Fomento Economico Mexicano (FEMSA) by buying 22 percent of its beer-brewing subsidiary, the maker of Dos Equis and Tecate brand beers. Each company will distribute the other's beer at home and jointly wage an assault on the U.S. market.

Cross-Border Alliances

McKinsey and Company studied success rates and factors for cross-border alliances. It found that the rate of success runs about 50 percent and that alliances tend to be most effective at helping firms edge into new related businesses or new geographic regions, while acquisitions work better for core business expansion.

McKinsey determined that alliances across borders often fail if they are unbalanced, that is, between partners of unequal size or skill, or if one partner has more at stake than the other. Success rates were quite good in cross-border alliances where partners were often equal in size or skill and where proceeds from the alliance partner's success were equally divided. Siemens' successful alliance with Corning via patents is held up as an example of two large, multiskilled firms that grew the fiber-optic cable business in Europe by sharing skills (Siemens—manufacturing and distribution skills—and Corning—R & D process patent skills).

McKinsey also found that cross-border alliances in which the partners demonstrated flexibility could flourish because they outrun the start-up issues that plague most cross-border alliances in the first two years of their life. Staying flexible overcomes start-up problems and disillusionments, and after these problems get resolved, the scope of alliances across borders often increases. General Electric's alliance with Snecma to originally develop and manufacture the CFM 56 jet engine grew to encompass a second series of CFM 6 engines, to the tune of 10,000 engine orders worth $39 billion in business.

One issue alliance partners must come to grips with is their preparedness to share "strategic" information. On the dimension of information sharing, many cultural differences exist. When the *Harvard Business Review* polled worldwide managers on their willingness to share strategic information with outsiders, it found Japanese managers very reticent, Germans fairly open, and American managers in-between. These low Japanese scores were explained by their penchant for mass production, tightly controlled by them, while Germans often sell specialized, customized products into markets requiring a more open culture of sharing.[4] American managers tend to share sometimes (on marketing/customer information) but covet information of a technology nature.

The Varying Levels of Complexity

While multiplayer alliances have been used to construct mega-merger projects, productive alliances needn't be complex. For instance, Baskin Robbins has opened ice cream counters in Wendy's fast food outlets, in a cooperative effort that helps both firms' sales. In other cases, firms such as Bloomingdales rent space to cosmetics firms such as Revlon in combinations that help the retailer build store traffic with suppliers that have considerably greater specific product knowledge. Similarly, magazines often partner to sell advertising with combined program offerings that give better value to their clients than individual offerings could provide.

Firms can ally on something as simple as a spot promotion that provides mutual synergy. Major movie studios promote specially priced movie series with other firms. In 1991, Paramount teamed up with McDonald's to promote its *Indiana Jones* video series for the special price of $7.99 per tape. The success of that effort spawned a series of such promotions for a number of movies such as *Batman* and *The Flintstones.*

As a growth vehicle, alliances offer tremendous variety in scope from limited-function collaborations on promotions or selling to very complex alliances involving entire new-generation product development or marketing. Of course, the more complex the product, the more complex the relationship. Because alliances do not involve equity purchases, they are essentially governed by agreement and kept on-track by mutual consent and gain. Successful alliances depend on a working chemistry between those individuals in each firm who actually do the work. The sense of partnership depends on the sense of mutually shared risk and gain; when one partner feels too much the junior, trust and commitment are far more difficult to build.

Case 12

Pope and Talbot and McKesson's Supply Chain Alliances: Powerful Marketing Engines for Growth

Strategic Alliances between companies in the supply chain can be very powerful vehicles for growth. Consider two cases in point: Pope & Talbot, an Oregon-based manufacturer of private label diapers and supermarket paper products which has strategic alliances with retailers such as Dominicks; and McKesson Drug Company, a wholesaler of drugs which has alliances with independent retail drug stores totaling more than 3,900 store locations.

By entering a strategic alliance with Dominicks to link their total supply chain processes (order replenishment, inventory forecasting, delivery, billing, bar coding stock, and lead time management), Pope and Talbot was able to achieve the following:

1. Save Dominicks 2.1 percent of sales in margins;
2. Reduce Dominicks' order lead time from weeks to 48 hours;
3. Reduce Dominicks' average inventory by two-thirds to one and a half weeks worth.

Pope and Talbot essentially plans and manages Dominicks' order replenishment system for private label diapers, paper towels, and bathroom and facial tissue. By linking their information systems, Pope and Talbot's factories and warehouses are driven by point-of-sale checkout scanner data transmitted on-line.

The Volvo-Renault alliance to share technology and facilities for making cars, trucks, buses and their components illustrates the need for mutuality of interest and the need for matched strategy. Volvo is strong in large car and gasoline engines in North America and Northern Europe. Renault is strong in small cars and diesel engines in Southern Europe and Latin America. In February 1990, they formed

In saving its alliance partner money, Pope and Talbot also saved 2.3 percent in margin that used to be eaten up by the costs of excess inventories, missed forecasts, higher raw material costs than necessary, and inopportune factory loading that resulted from the previously unlinked systems. The company has grown to be the dominant private label diaper supplier in this $400 million segment of the business.[5]

McKesson grew its business to over $9 billion (+15%) in 1993 by supply chain alliances with independent pharmacies it services. When an independent drugstore signs an alliance with McKesson for its wholesale drug needs, it gets a full range of services including:

- Electronic data exchange on billings/orders and price-ticketing services;
- A full range of advertising programs (12 per year) that it can tailor for its use; and
- Service via McKesson's Acumax system, the most automated, accurate, low cost warehousing system in the world. The system uses light-weight arm-mounted computers on pickers that scan bar codes for workers who pick items as they are scanned in sequence. McKesson's technology is so powerful that it can pick orders faster and more accurately than any wholesaler in any line of business in North America.

McKesson won 600 new drug store customers in 1992 alone, boosting its independents from 3,300 to 3,900 across the U.S.

---

an alliance to cooperate in product design, purchasing, transportation, components making, and safety research and development.[6] Eventually the alliance led the firms into formal merger proposals, which collapsed when Volvo's board refused to merge. The bitterness that flowed from the failed merger talks also led to dissolution of the alliance after three years and the resignation of Volvo's CEO.

The Growth Masters—Alliances

Company	***Product***	***Market***
Merck/DuPont	Pharmaceuticals	Business
Nestlé	Food	Consumer
Apple Computer/Sony	Computers	Consumer/Business
Coca-Cola/Cadbury Schweppes	Soft Drinks	Consumer
Pilkington Glass	Glass	Business
Bell Atlantic	Communications	Consumer/Business
Eli Lilly	Pharmaceuticals	Business
Rhone Poulenc Rorer	Pharmaceuticals	Business
SmithKline Beecham	Pharmaceuticals	Business
Anheuser Busch	Beverages	Consumer
Corning/Siemens	Fiber Optics	Business
General Electric/Snecma	Jet Engines	Business
Pope & Talbot	Paper Products	Consumer/Business
McKesson	Wholesale Drugs	Business

"Virtual" Alliances

Some management thinkers believe alliances will one day be so common on so many fronts—with outsourced preferred product suppliers, with key customers, with competitors, with complementary business partners, and with specialized services providers—that it will be difficult to determine where one company ends and the other begins.[7] These "virtual corporations" or "relationship enterprises" span different countries, industries, and technologies through a network of agreements, held together only by common goals and complementary visions that come and go as opportunities do. These types of firms are so unlike most companies they appear "unreal" (hence the descriptor "virtual" to describe their boundaryless impermanence and continuous transformation). While it's no doubt true that novel alliances are gaining acceptance as companies seek to co-produce value in different ways, alliances as a replacement for traditional corporations are unrealistic, since such alliances cannot anchor employees in value-bonding cultures of ongoing permanence. Boundaryless organizations are problematic to staff and finance on any ongoing, long-term basis since neither employees nor shareholders know what the entity stands for.

Joint Ventures: Growth by Establishing a Separate Organization

Somewhere between the looseness of alliances and the total control of acquisitions is the use of joint venturing for growth. In joint venture arrangements, firms set up a separate, formal entity usually in order to exploit some new opportunity, such as a new market or technology. Each partner has a formal equity position in the entity.

Corning Glass is one of the world's preeminent firms using this growth tactic. Its joint ventures comprise half of its sales and a significant share of its earnings. In most cases, its joint venture company is exploiting some technology related to silica (the raw material of glass), Corning's core technology. Dow-Corning, its joint venture with Dow Chemical, exploits silicone, a silica derivative, while Owens-Corning, another joint venture, exploits silica in fiberglass form in "Pink" insulation. Inaki Glass, which Corning formed in Japan with Asahi Glass, exploits Corning patents on silica products.

For a research and development-driven firm such as Corning (inventors of fiber optics), joint venture companies are a great way to gain market access and production capacity faster and less expensively than outright acquisition. Alliances, which Corning also uses, are somewhat riskier in terms of knowledge transfer. The formal legal structure of a joint venture company limits access to Corning's proprietary research and development secrets and also gives the company a clearly defined ownership interest and thus greater control.

Joint Ventures with Minority Interests

While many of Corning's joint ventures are 50-50 equity propositions, joint ventures for growth needn't involve equal interests. Effective bonding and sharing of resources to exploit skills profitably doesn't require a 50-50 stake. Ford owns 25 percent of Mazda and shares car designs and joint factory capacity. Mazda's Flat Rock, Michigan, plant produces Ford's Probe as well as Mazda models. Initially, Mazda used Ford's 25 percent ownership stock purchase to help finance rotary engine development, and Ford used the venture to increase vehicle production capacity. As the Japanese yen grew in value, it began to make more sense for Ford to supply Mazda's needs and less sense for Ford to source from Mazda, Japan. Hence, Ford and Mazda began joint production in America.

Thanks to the joint venture, both companies have stronger product lines, lower costs, and better quality. Executives at Ford and Mazda (which highly prizes its independence) both believe these benefits in growth and productivity would not have been any better if Ford had acquired Mazda or if the joint venture had been 50-50 rather than 25-75. As the two partners share and grow, each benefits from the other's growth while still retaining independence of action and entrepreneurship, qualities often destroyed by outright acquisition. Minority joint ventures provide growth momentum while preserving each partner's operating culture and vitality.

Joint Ventures for Services

Ogilvy & Mather, a global advertising and public relations giant, bought 30 percent of Charles E. Walker, a public lobbying firm in Washington, D.C. As a result of their agreement, Ogilvy refers its ad clients in need of lobbying help to Walker, while Walker refers its lobbying clients to Ogilvy when they need grass-roots public relations. Each firm has piggybacked the other's client list for growth. Ogilvy also helps Walker by referring its European clients who have lobbying needs in Europe—enabling Walker to grow its lobbying practice in Europe.

All of this is occurring despite the fact that Ogilvy & Mather's 30 percent stake carries no voting rights. The joint venture's success hinges almost entirely on the referral linkages between the firms. Neither firm saw any reason for a parity 50-50 stake since each exploits the other's contacts based on opportunity and joint projects that are typically not a 50-50 proposition. The equity stake allows Ogilvy to hold some sway with Walker, but for the most part they grow together through shared opportunism that is not always equal on a revenue flow basis. In fact, the terms of the pact dictate that Ogilvy's dividends of 30 percent are cut if Walker generates a lot of direct business for Ogilvy; in addition, each exchanges finder's fees routinely, despite their equity partnership.[8]

Joint Ventures and Global Branding

As some industries globalize, often an independent finds it tougher to succeed. This is the case in the hotel industry, where global chains such as Hilton, Trusthouse Forte, and others dominate. As a result, independents often form joint ventures and merge. In Canada, for instance, Journey's End has struck up a joint venture with Choice Hotels International, a U.S. hotel giant. The new company, called Choice Hotels Canada, Inc., combines 120 Journey's End properties with 54 Choice Hotels in Canada to become Canada's largest chain hotel franchise. The joint venture is expected to lower operating costs and boost marketing muscle in an increasingly competitive market.

Joint Ventures: Avoiding the Thorns among the Roses

While joint venture companies can represent less cost and trauma than acquisition and can afford more influence and control than "softer" alliances, making them work is not easy.

AT&T formed a minority joint venture with Olivetti by buying 23.5 percent of Olivetti's stock. The idea was that Olivetti would help AT&T penetrate telecommunication markets in Europe, while AT&T would help Olivetti sell its computers in the U.S. The grand vision was for these two firms to combine technologies to take on IBM. The venture collapsed when each realized that the other did not have the skills it expected.

Hechinger, an East Coast home improvement chain, formed a joint venture with Kmart to develop a nationwide chain of do-it-yourself stores, but the venture collapsed when neither could agree on basic store layouts, merchandising, staffing, and advertising. The venture ended, and Kmart eventually formed its own chain of do-it-yourself centers—Builders Square.

As evidenced by these examples, joint ventures can founder for a variety of operating, philosophical, and skill expectation deficiencies.

The Growth Masters—Joint Ventures

Company	*Product*	*Market*
Corning/Dow Chemical	Silicone	Consumer
Corning/Asahi Glass	Glass	Consumer/Business
Ford/Mazda	Automobiles	Consumer
Ogilvy & Mather/Charles E. Walker	Public Relations	Business
Journey's End/Choice Hotels	Hotels	Consumer/Business

It takes real patience, perseverance, and astute partner selection to figure out whether or not a joint venture can work in practice, not just on paper, where so many alliances "look" good.

In the NUMMI joint venture between Toyota and General Motors, General Motors thought it would learn Toyota's just-in-time methods up close and transfer them to its General Motors plants worldwide. Toyota, on the other hand, hoped it would learn how to work with American employees and suppliers. Toyota learned quickly, increasing its U.S. market share, but General Motors learned more slowly. Its interest in the relationship languished and fell as it faced deep-seated internal resistance to Toyota style and methods, which require high levels of employee trust. This failed joint venture illustrates the difficulty of deriving mutual benefit from joint ventures. To work successfully, joint ventures must mesh culturally as well as operationally. Joint venture partners who don't do their homework on each other's cultures can end up "like a miserably married couple, living as strangers under the same roof."[9]

Summary

Collaboration is a watchword of contemporary business, and the various "outreach" strategies discussed in this chapter show that cooperation between and among firms can provide profitable growth for all parties involved. Whether by outright acquisition, the formation of strategic alliances, or the creation of joint ventures, companies can develop structures that enhance the potential for quality growth at minimal risk. While these three strategies are fraught with risk, if done wisely, as Corning, Ford and Newell Company clearly demonstrate, they can boost growth and productive earnings for years to come.

Notes

1. Peter Fuhrman, "Here Comes House Music," *Forbes,* Dec. 21, 1992: 44–46.
2. *The Economist,* August 22, 1992: 61–62, "The NonConformist," Management brief by the editors of *The Economist.*
3. *The Economist,* Feb. 6, 1993: 69, "The Global Firm R.I.P.," in Management Focus column, by the editors of *The Economist.*
4. Tom Peters, "The Boundaries of Business Partners, the Rhetoric and Reality," *Harvard Business Review,* Sept.–Oct. 1991: 97–99.
5. *Private Label Magazine,* Nov./Dec. 1993: 157–158, "Pope & Talbot Implements Supply Chain Management," by the editors.
6. Julie Cohen Mason, Case Study: "The Marriage of Volvo and Renault," *Management Review,* May 1993: 12.
7. John Byrne, Richard Brandt and Otis Port, "The Virtual Corporation," *Business Week,* Feb. 8, 1993.
8. For a full explanation of the Ogilvy-Walker equity venture, see Jordan D. Lewis, "Partners for Profit," New York: Free Press, 1990: 109, 112, 120, 121.
9. Anne B. Fisher, "How to Make a Merger Work," *Fortune,* Jan. 24, 1994: 68.

Epilogue

The Growth Masters

I would say the nineties are a decade without mercy.

Philip Kotler
Northwestern University
Interview Feb. 1994
in *Canadian Business*

Firms are always seeking new "risk free" ways to grow—the perpetual dream of all corporate treasurers. For instance, banks reeling from losses in real estate or third world loans or credit card operations are trying to migrate to lower-risk growth options, such as providing private banking to wealthy individuals or selling transaction processing, cash management, or securities custody services. But, of course, the nineties and *risk free* may not be words that fit together.

The nineties represent a singularly harsher economic landscape than the last five decades. On *Business Week*'s 1992 "Top 500 International Corporations" listing, one-quarter of all firms *lost* money. While some of this profit is cyclical in nature, some is not, and global supply will likely exceed demand for some time (or global prices will remain soft for many years). The implication, of course, is clear: growth must come from all avenues except price increases. This book has isolated 18 ways to grow without higher prices. Each of these varies in risk and complexity. Acquisitions are a great growth strategy, but they can be traumatic and risky. Product line extensions are low in complexity, low in risk, but they may also be low in impact unless real "world-beating" line extensions are created such as "Diet Coke" (now almost as good a seller as Regular Coke). In the middle of the risk/complexity grid would be market expansion strategies, the pursuit of new users, usages and neglected geographic parts of the market. (See Exhibit E–1.)

It is probably necessary for firms in the nineties to pursue multiple growth vectors simultaneously. Otherwise, meaningful growth will simply not occur. Such pressures, of course, will require companies to learn to use unfamiliar growth strategies never considered before, or considered but rejected because of risk or complexity. For instance, Apple[1] is trying licensing (its technology) for the first time, because their growth has slowed and it must pursue a new way to grow. Pella,[2]

Exhibit E–1
A Matrix of Growth Strategies Contrasting Their Degrees of Risk/Capability Stretch

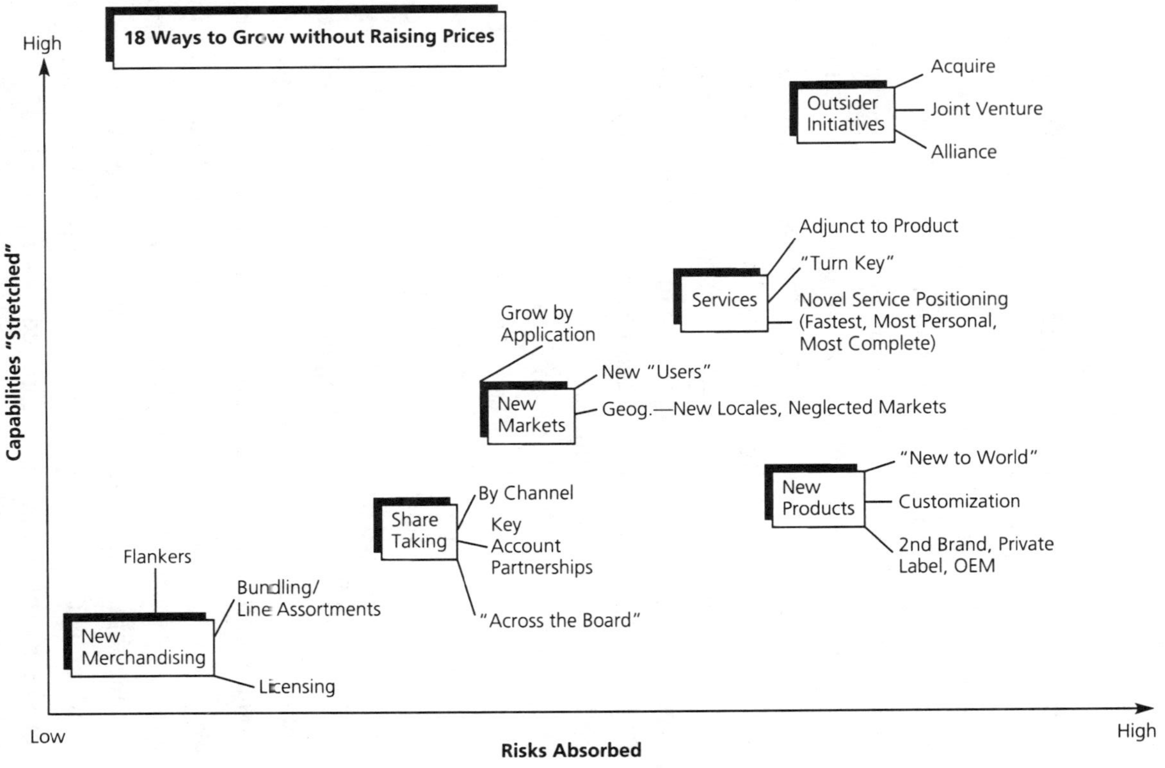

the privately held 68-year-old window manufacturer, is learning to grow via brand portfolio expansion. For 37 straight years prior to 1988, sales growth grew at 9 percent compounded rates. Then growth stopped. The market, which had always welcomed Pella's high-end windows, balked at prices fewer home builders could afford. So the company launched a broader brand portfolio including a second brand line, the "Pro-Line," 12 to 20 percent less expensive than its premium "Designer Window" Series. And Pella is now selling through channels (another new growth vector) it hasn't used before—Home Depot and Pay Less Cashways—mass market home supply outlets versus its traditional 369 exclusive Pella distributors. Interestingly, to placate its dealers, who were miffed at the new strategy, Pella pays an override sales commission to distributors, based on the mass market builder supply outlets' sales in their area. In exchange for this commission Pella asks the distributors to train these chains (such as Home Depot) on how to sell Pella windows and to help with some installations of the lower priced Pro-Line sold to builders. Revenue growth (and profits) have bounced back as Pella has begun to master these two new growth strategies.

When J.C. Penney's revenues went flat and its profits dropped 28 percent, it realized it needed a new growth strategy. So it more strongly committed to private label brands (it had always had private label underwear and towels) in upscale but sound-value apparel for professional women. It hired designers, assigned fashion-smart brand managers, and created a whole "look" to go along with new brand names—Worthington and Stafford—and its value pricing (versus competitors such as Dayton-Hudson, The Gap, Mervyn's, etc.). The result of learning to use this growth strategy is that Penney's sales were up 11 percent and profits improved by 47 percent (1993 versus 1992). As Penney's CEO William Howell stated, "We didn't sit and defend ourselves, we went to work and we said we've got to change. We made private brands our competitive advantage."[3]

The Key to Strategy Selection

This book has emphasized the importance of firms using multiple platforms to grow. Historic reliance on a single strategy or a couple of growth platforms no longer works. So McDonald's cannot count on just adding new outlets or new menus to grow; it has to chase entirely new types of user locations—on army bases, universities, in hospitals, and so forth. Disney can't just grow through theme parks and movies to meet its targets. It needs added services, such as its hotels, resort facilities, retail stores, and book, record, video publishing businesses.

Within industries, the possibility of rivals pursuing radically different strategies from each other and all still growing is also feasible. And nowhere is this phenomenon better illustrated than in the management consulting industry. Management consultants around the world billed $17 billion in advice in 1993, according to *Consultant's News,* an industry newsletter, up 10 percent from 1992. About $8.1 billion of this was accounted for by the industry's top 10 players—each of which grew *at or above* the industry's growth rate with quite different growth strategies.

McKinsey and Co. of New York grows by tapping the high end of the market. It is the pricey company of its peers, billing an average about $420,000 per consultant per year (with 3,200 consultants worldwide). So McKinsey has a very tight focus by project—attacking the market for strategy related advice—and going for major projects.

This growth strategy is dramatically different than that used by another successful firm—Anderson Consulting of Chicago. Anderson uses almost ten times the number of the consultants as McKinsey, goes for market share globally (vs. a focused segment), and takes on more, smaller projects—often with an information systems slant, the company's historic roots. In 1993, Anderson consultants' billing averaged $127,822 (22,500 consultants), only about one-third of McKinsey's average.

Other players such as CSC Index, The Monitor Group, and BCG—all of Boston—are niche players, building on a particular expertise in new "big think" management concepts. CSC Index is the world's leader in re-engineering. Its CEO, Jim Champy, co-authored the bestseller *Re-engineering the Corporation* with Mike Hammer. Monitor's consulting niche has been built on Michael Porter's (of Harvard) ideas about strategy. BCG, originators of the "Experience Curve" strategy models, has expanded its practice into new concepts such as time-based competition, via George Stalk, author of a book on the subject. Stalk is a key BCG principal.

Two other successful consulting organizations have grown, not by product specialization but by merger or acquisition. Mercer Management Consulting of New York is the combination of three firms: Temple, Barker & Sloane; Strategic Planning Associates; and Marsh & McLennan. Similarly, Gemini Consulting in Morristown, New York, is the combination of the MAC Group and United Research Company.

Cooper & Lybrand, with more than 7,600 consultants and more than $1.3 billion in revenue, pursues yet another growth strategy. It sells expertise in four widely different areas—cost reduction, information systems, strategy, and process re-engineering. Its skills, of course, grew from its original business as a "BIG 8" accounting firm.

So while all good consultants chase "name" clients (Fortune 500 firms) and all operate in most major cities around the world, their growth strategies are radically different yet all successful. McKinsey goes for the high-priced, large-project client. Anderson goes for the mass market. Cooper's sells multiple competencies, while others (BCG, Monitor, CSC Index) are more narrow in their consulting practice specializations. Still others have grown by buying or merging their firms with allies.

The message is clear from this diversity of growth strategies: There is no single way to grow in an industry. Many approaches *can* and *do* succeed simultaneously. Making the most of opportunities means deciding which particular growth vector suits a firm's core competencies and "comfort" by market. This size-up of opportunities matched to skills requires excellent leadership. All firms are faced with threats to their continued prosperity and growth, whether from competitive displacement or the decline in potency of their core product lines/ services. It is how these threats are managed and how well a firm's leadership charts various growth paths through the inevitable morass of obstacles that separates the outstanding leadership from the mediocre. As Arnold Toynbee pointed out in his classic *Study of History,* all civilizations can either survive and prosper or decline, depending on whether strong leaders come forth to meet the challenges presented to them.

This process of "challenge and response" is dynamic: No single growth strategy works all of the time or for all time, and it is top management's role to bet on and emphasize those growth platforms that will keep the firm proactive and self-renewing despite discontinuous change. An excellent example of a management team that has demonstrated this ability is Hewlett-Packard. Their beginnings harken back to the 1930s as a manufacturer of video oscillators and electrical testing equipment. Yet today despite radical changes in technology, rivals, markets, and customers, H-P leads the world in precision plotters, laser printers, computer workstations, professional calculators, and medical analytic devices—all growth products unimagined even twenty years ago. Kodak, on the other hand, has not plotted its growth pathways as cleverly, nor have IBM, Sears, General Motors, Digital Equipment, which bet on growth platforms that either lacked continued vitality or a realistic fit to core skills. As a result, they have paid dearly for their lost vitality in job dislocation, financial write-downs, loss of shareholder value, and ongoing problems of customer and investor confidence.

Real Growth Masters

There are outstanding growth-mastering companies facing up to the decade's tougher economic realities and learning to grow by adding several new strategies to their dominant historical patterns. Their learning as corporations is in many senses broad-spectrum versus narrow, a multiskilled approach to their own reinvention as corporations. It is these companies I would call "Growth Masters" since their momentum has been energized from a number of platforms all working in concert for growth. In their corporate consciences, these firms seem to live Theodore Levitt's prophetic words that "in truth there is no such thing as a growth industry . . . there are only companies organized and operated to create and capitalize on growth opportunities."[4]

Three great examples of Growth Masters are: The Walt Disney Company, Loctite Corporation, and Crompton and Knowles.

Walt Disney Company historically used three dominant growth strategies: theme park geographic expansion, licensing of Disney characters, and the search for new Disney customers for its films and television shows. What Disney has done marvelously well is expand on each of these. To its theme parks it has added services, such as resort hotels, vacation time-sharing real estate tie-ins, and an attraction alliance with MGM (in Europe) at its EuroDisney site. To its traditional growth vector of market expansion in television and films it has added new products such as home video, its own Disney channel on pay television, and software developed with Nintendo. To its licensing umbrella have been added an entire book publishing division, Disney retail stores, and a Disney magazine. And all the while Disney is boosting its theme parks with new attractions to revitalize them. (Mickey's Toontown in Anaheim; in France Disney is spending $100 million to add rides; while Disney Tokyo is looking at a whole new "Disney Sea" maritime park addition.) Its new projects since 1987 have generated $1.7 billion, almost as much revenue as its entire theme park division generated in 1987 ($1.8 billion). So Disney clearly is a far more skilled growth diversifier than it was just a few short years ago. It has driven change, not just managed it. And while the company has not succeeded 100 percent with every new growth strategy (for instance EuroDisney), it is continuing to experiment with new growth platforms.

Loctite Corporation is another growth mastering firm. In 1984 its sales were $284 million and its overseas business was 40 percent of the firm. Its sales were growing but not by great leaps and bounds. And while its dominant growth strategy has involved lots of new products, its industrial sealants and adhesives were not anywhere near as pervasive as they could be in various different markets.

The company has decided to expand its growth vectors to include customer partnerships with key accounts, finding new user industries, and broadening its approach to new locales. It developed customized adhesives for auto makers and electronics manufacturers. It shifted some market emphasis to selling to aftermarket maintenance departments versus its traditional focus on original equipment manufacturers' use of its products. And it expanded overseas into Hungary, Czechoslovakia, Poland, Singapore, Taiwan—a total of more than 80 nations—so that its sales overseas are today 60 percent of its mix. And what has it got to show for its efforts? Sales today are more than $600 million, and profits have risen from $17 million (on $240 million in 1984) to in excess of $72 million, putting Loctite in the Fortune 500.

Crompton and Knowles is yet a third example of a masterful growth company. More than a decade ago (1982) its sales were $135 million and its profits $5 million, or 3 percent of sales. Its return on equity was 7.6 percent and sales per employee were at $108,000. In 1992 its revenues exceeded $517 million, its growth continued to $578 million (1993) and profits were seven times its decade-earlier level, at $35 million. Its margin of profits to sales has improved from 3 percent to 8 percent; its return on equity is 27 percent and its sales per employee are $237,000.

How did a small manufacturer of industrial dyes, food ingredients, and plastics extruders for wiring and cable do this when growth in all of its primary markets was flat? Its primary growth strategies have always been share taking, geographic expansion, and the development of new products. It has leading market shares in dyes for carpet, dyes for leather, and dyes for paper mills, all markets not growing very much. Crompton and Knowles has always invested heavily in new products with 20 percent of its sales in products developed in the last five years. In addition the company has always emphasized sales and manufacturing in Europe and Asia, including a joint venture to produce its dyes in Thailand. What Crompton and Knowles has done in recent years is to utilize much more heavily three different growth strategies: a deeper commitment to customer partnerships; a more aggressive search for new user industries for its products; and, lastly, a heightened use of acquisition for market share in selected markets.

In terms of customer partnerships, Crompton and Knowles has recognized that its food company customers have cut back their research and design spending and have turned with increased interest to companies such as Crompton and Knowles for proprietary development of new flavor or sweetening ingredients that suit microwave cooking, shelf stable foods, and new nutritional lifestyles (such as microwaveable rice and MSG-free snack foods). These partnerships include companies such as Grand Met Foodservice, whose new biscuits include a proprietary flavor ingredient from Crompton and Knowles. Other partners include Quaker Oats and Pillsbury.

In Crompton and Knowles' search for new user industries it has found customers for its specialty chemicals in pharmaceuticals (flavor coatings for oral medicines) and new customers for plastic extrusion equipment in childrens' toys and furniture, medical tubing, and recyclers of plastics.

In addition, it has acquired several firms to add to its sales and production base, including ICI's pre-metallized dye plant in France and Atlantic Industries' dye operation in Nutley, New Jersey. In the specialty extrusion business it acquired Sterling which alone accounted for a $30 million sales gain in 1991 year end.

Summary

Each of these masterful growth firms has shown flexibility in managing, as their markets have flattened out (even Disney's theme park attendance is only increasing 3 percent per year)[5] and each has been prepared to absorb the new risks that altered strategies demand. These twin characteristics of courage and nimbleness have distinguished their managements. For in the turbulence and trauma of the nineties, it will take multiple strategies to secure growth from competitors. The 18 platforms for growth outlined in this book provide a pathway to higher sales and earnings. But it still takes skilled and insightful leadership to climb onto the platforms, and use them as springboards for success.

Notes

1. *Sales and Marketing Management,* July 1993: 25, "Apple's About-Face," no author cited.
2. Ronald Henkoff, "Pella Moving Up by Downscaling," *Fortune,* August 9, 1993: 72.
3. Zina Moukheiber, "Our Competitive Advantage," a profile of J.C. Penney's new growth strategy, *Forbes,* April 12, 1993: 60.
4. *Harvard Business Review,* Sept./Oct. 1975: 28. This prophetic quote was made eighteen years earlier in 1975 by Levitt in Marketing Myopia.
5. R. Grover, S. Toy, G. DeGeorge, R. Neff, "Thrills and Chills at Disney," *Business Week,* June 21, 1993: 73, 74.

Index